The Best Of *The Mailbox*®
Science
Primary

Explore the wonder and beauty of science with *The Best Of* The Mailbox® *Science.* This compilation of teaching units—selected from 1989 to 1996 issues of *The Mailbox*® magazine for primary teachers—will energize your science lessons and strengthen students' science skills. Inside this invaluable classroom resource, you'll find:

- Science-based thematic units with across-the-curriculum activities
- Background information
- Helpful ideas for science centers
- Experiments
- Independent and small-group activities
- Critical-thinking activities
- Literature links
- Reproducibles
- Patterns

Editors:
Diane Badden
Sharon Murphy

Artists:
Pam Crane
Teresa Davidson
Susan Hodnett
Rebecca Saunders
Barry Slate

Cover Artist:
Jennifer Tipton Bennett

www.themailbox.com

Table Of Contents

Manufactured in the United States
10 9 8 7 6 5 4

A Pocketful Of Science

Practicing The Basics

Supply your budding scientists with some of the basic skills they'll need to "do science" all year long!

ideas by Ann Flagg

Activity 1: Observing Buttons

You will need:
five buttons
five 12" x 18" sheets of white construction paper
markers
glue

What to do:
Introduce your collection of five buttons; then choose one button from the batch. Ask students to *observe* the button and describe its *properties* or characteristics. List the students' observations on a sheet of construction paper. (See the illustration.) When the list is complete, glue the corresponding button to the top of the poster and title the poster "Properties Of This Button." Repeat the activity until a poster has been created for each button.

Questions to ask:
1. Can a button have more than one property?
2. How did you discover the properties of each button?
3. Which of the five senses were important to your observations?

This is why:

The ability to observe is fundamental to science. Observing involves using one or more of the five senses to learn more about objects and events. Scientists use their five senses to gather information about the world around them.

Activity 2: Classifying Buttons

You will need:
ten buttons for each small group of students
posters completed in Activity 1

What to do:
Review the button-property posters from Activity 1 with your students. Next divide students into small groups and give each group ten buttons. Ask each group to observe its button collection for common properties, then determine a means for *classifying* or grouping its collection into two sets. Ask each group to share its classification rule. Then allow time for the groups to reclassify their collections using a variety of classification rules.

Questions to ask:
1. Can buttons be classified in more than one way?
2. What kinds of things can be classified?
3. How do you think scientists use classification?

This is why:

Scientists use classification to group and sort the information that they gather. Classification ranges from the simple grouping of objects or events based on common properties to the more complex categorizing based on existing relationships between objects or events.

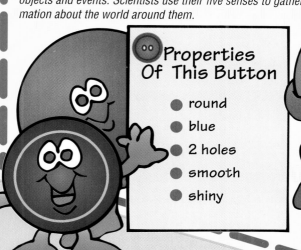

Properties Of This Button
- round
- blue
- 2 holes
- smooth
- shiny

Follow-up:
Have students complete the activity on page 5.

Pam Crane

Activity 3: Predicting Outcomes

You will need:

three large ice cubes
clear plastic tumbler
cookie sheet
pitcher of water
blank paper: one sheet per student
timer

What to do:

Under the watchful eyes of your students, lay the cookie sheet on a tabletop. Set the plastic tumbler on the cookie sheet and place the ice cubes in the tumbler. Then completely fill the tumbler with water. Ask students to describe their observations. Next ask each student to ponder what might happen when the ice cubes melt. After several possibilities have been brainstormed, have each student write or draw his prediction on a sheet of paper. Set the timer for 20 minutes.

When the timer sounds, direct your students' attention to the tumbler. Give the students a chance to observe the tumbler, the water, and the ice cubes; then ask them to describe any changes they observe. Explain that scientists often alter their predictions based on new observations. Encourage all students to reevaluate their predictions based on their latest observations and make any desired changes. Then reset the timer. Continue in this manner until the ice cubes have completely melted.

Questions to ask:
1. What happened when the ice melted?
2. Did the ice take up space in the water? Explain your answer.

This is why:

Since ice is less dense than water, parts of the ice cubes float above the waterline. Because of this, students often predict that the tumbler will overflow when the ice cubes melt. However, since water (ice) expands at 32° Fahrenheit, ice takes up slightly more space than water does. In this demonstration, the tumbler does not overflow because the water from the melted ice fills the space left by the ice. In fact, although it may be difficult to observe, the water level will be slightly lower after the ice melts.

Activity 4: Testing Predictions

For each small group of students, you will need:

sheet of blank paper
pencil
pitcher of water
clear plastic tumbler
three large ice cubes
aluminum pie pan
paper towels

What to do:

Write the following question on the chalkboard: "What will happen if three ice cubes are added to a full glass of water?" Divide students into small groups. Ask each group to discuss the question and predict a possible answer. Disburse the supplies listed above and ask one person in each group to record his group's prediction. Next challenge each group to create and complete a science experience to test its prediction.

Questions to ask:
1. How did your experience test your prediction?
2. Did you find it necessary to change your prediction during the course of the experience?
3. What did you learn?
4. At any time during this activity, did you use any information that you learned in a previous science experience?

This is why:

The water in the glass will overflow because—unlike Activity 3—the ice was added to a full glass of water. Students will once again see that ice takes up space. Remind students that predicting requires proposing possible outcomes of future events based upon observations and inferences drawn from previous events.

For the teacher:

Many children are uncomfortable making predictions because of their desire to give the "right" answers. During this and other science experiences, try to show students that you are interested in their learning and thinking processes, rather than the correctness of their answers. It is important that students realize that to a scientist, an experience that nullifies a prediction can yield as much or more information as an experience that verifies a prediction.

Name _____

Classification Challenge

Follow these steps:

☐ Color and cut out the picture cards below.

☐ Carefully study the pictures.

☐ Sort the pictures into sets.

☐ Remember that each set must have a common property.

☐ Glue the sets onto a sheet of construction paper.

☐ Name each set.

After you finish each step, color the small box.

Note To Teacher: Use this activity after completing "Activity 2: Classifying Buttons" on page 3. Each student needs a 9" x 12" sheet of construction paper, crayons, scissors, and glue. Accept all reasonable classifications.

MIND OVER MATTER

Getting A Grip On The Basics Of Matter

So what's the matter? Has the thought of teaching your students the basics of matter turned you topsy-turvy? If that's the case, then it's time to get a grip—on matter, that is! Use this collection of hands-on activities and teaching ideas to help students understand that *matter* really matters!

ideas by Sue Boulais and Ann Flagg

Learning About Matter

Give meaning to matter with this simple classroom activity. Tell students that matter is anything that takes up space and has weight; then challenge them to find matter within the classroom. After each child has named at least one item, ask students to survey the room again—but this time looking for items that are *not* matter. Guide students to determine that almost everything that can be seen and touched is matter.

What About Air?

Air is matter—though youngsters may find this idea difficult to grasp. These quick demonstrations will help students get a grip on air. Ask each child to place her palms on her chest as she takes a few deep breaths. Have a student describe what happens to her chest when she breathes in air. *(It expands to make room for the air.)* Next have students observe you inflating a balloon. This time ask students what is inside the balloon. *(Air.)* Lastly capture some air inside a plastic produce bag; then seal the bag with a twist tie. Ask questions like "What do you see inside the bag?" and "How do you know something is inside the bag?" To further illustrate that air takes up space, place the inflated bag on a table and balance a book or other solid object atop it. Ask students to describe what is keeping the object from touching the table.

Taking Up Space

This small-group activity makes it clear that not all things take up space. Give each small group of students a permanent marker, a golf ball, and a large plastic cup half-filled with water. Ask one student in each group to draw a line on the outside of his group's cup to mark the water level. (This reading should be taken at eye level.) Then ask each group to predict what will happen when a golf ball is placed in the cup. When the predictions are made, have one student from each group gently drop a golf ball into the group's cup. Then ask another student in each group to mark the new water level. Discuss how this activity proves that a golf ball is matter. *(It takes up space.)* Then ask students if they think *light* is matter. In turn, shine a flashlight on each cup of water. Allow time for the groups to check their water levels, then take a vote—is light matter? Students will see firsthand that because light does not take up space, it is not matter. (Examples of other things that are not matter are sound, shadows, thoughts, feelings, and dreams.)

Matter Really Matters

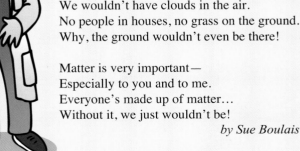

Matter is very important;
It makes up the things that we see.
Without it, all things as we know them
Would simply just not even be!

We wouldn't have fish in the ocean;
We wouldn't have clouds in the air.
No people in houses, no grass on the ground.
Why, the ground wouldn't even be there!

Matter is very important—
Especially to you and to me.
Everyone's made up of matter…
Without it, we just wouldn't be!

by Sue Boulais

Properties Of Matter

When you explore properties of matter with the ever popular pogs, be warned—your students could go "pog" wild! For this activity each child needs a pog, paper, a pencil, and crayons. Explain that scientists describe matter using physical properties such as weight, color, hardness, shape, and size. When applicable, scientists also describe matter by its taste and smell. To begin have each child list physical properties of his pog. Encourage students to list properties that would help other scientists differentiate their pogs from the rest of the pogs. Next collect the papers and the pogs. Redistribute the papers, making sure that each student receives a paper other than his own; then scatter the pogs on a tabletop. In turn have small groups of students approach the table and try to identify the pogs described on the papers they hold. When a student thinks he has a match, he consults the classmate who created his list of properties. If the classmate does not confirm his pog identification, the student keeps looking. When most of the pogs have been identified, ask students to describe the properties that most pogs share. Also find out why they think some pogs are more difficult to identify than others. Then if desired display the pogs at a center. Students who visit the center can sort and classify the pogs by common properties.

Matter In A Bag

Solid, liquid, or gas? This partner activity has students identifying physical states of matter. Prepare a matter bag for every two students by placing different matter in each of several resealable plastic bags. (Inflate a few bags with air to represent gases. For liquids consider tinting water in a variety of colors. Be sure to avoid any liquids that might stain in the event of an accidental spill.) You will also need two or three sets of balance scales displayed around the room. Pair students and give each twosome a matter bag, a copy of the gameboard on page 11, and a game marker. Demonstrate how to use the gameboard; then let the fun begin. When pairs identify their matter, have them trade matter bags with other pairs who are finished and repeat the activity.

Solid, Liquid, *And* Gas?

Up to this point, students probably haven't considered that matter can change states or forms. For example a solid can become a liquid, and vice versa. This quick demonstration shows students how a solid turns into a liquid and then into a gas! Gather students around a preheated electric skillet. Students should be able to observe the skillet, but not touch it. Place an ice cube in the center of the skillet. As the ice melts, ask students to describe what is happening to the solid matter in the skillet. Then, as the liquid matter begins to boil and *steam,* ask the students what is happening to the matter. Conclude the demonstration when all evidence of the matter is gone. Challenge students to ponder other examples of changing matter in their everyday lives.

More Changing Matter

Students see three states of matter in this exciting demonstration. Using a funnel, pour vinegar (a liquid!) into a two-liter soda bottle. Stop pouring when the level of vinegar rises above the bottle's plastic base. Remove the funnel and set the bottle aside. Wipe the funnel clean; then use it to pour baking soda into a large balloon. When the balloon is half-full of baking soda, remove the funnel. Walk around the room and ask students to feel the lower half of the balloon—verifying that the matter inside is a solid. Then, being careful not to spill the baking soda into the bottle, secure the neck of the balloon over the bottle's mouth. When the balloon is securely attached to the bottle, lift the rest of the balloon over the bottle, causing the baking soda to drop into the two-liter bottle and the vinegar. Give the balloon momentary support as a resulting chemical reaction produces a gas inside the bottle and quickly inflates the balloon. What a *gas!*

7

Amazing Matter

Youngsters are sure to enjoy concocting these two recipes. The mixtures are unique because each one has properties of both solids and liquids. Lead students to understand that these types of matter are very difficult for scientists to categorize—but lots of fun for students to make! After each recipe is made, have students conduct a series of tests (see "Testing, Testing" below) on the resulting mixture to see if they can determine whether each substance is most like a liquid or a solid.

Solquid

Each student needs:
a paper-covered work space
a 9-oz. plastic cup
4 tablespoons of cornstarch
2 tablespoons of water
a wooden craft stick

Combine the cornstarch and the water in the plastic cup. Stir the mixture with the craft stick. The mixture should appear to be solidifying. If it does not, stir in a bit more cornstarch; then remove the craft stick. When the stick is removed, the substance should appear to be a liquid. But when the mixture is poked, stirred, or handled, it has properties of a solid.

Goop

Each student needs:
a paper-covered work space
a 9-oz. plastic cup
1 tablespoon of liquid starch
2 tablespoons of white glue
food coloring (optional)
a wooden craft stick

Combine the liquid starch, glue, and food coloring in the plastic cup. Stir until well mixed; then let the mixture stand for approximately five minutes. Stir the mixture again and let it stand for five more minutes. Repeat the stir-and-stand process once more; then handle the goop and enjoy its properties.

- Pour the mixture from one hand to another. What happens?
- Poke the mixture with your finger or the craft stick. What happens?
- Roll the mixture into a ball; then try to hold the ball. What happens?

Testing, Testing

Encourage students to use these methods and others of their own to test the properties of Solquid and Goop. Are these substances solids or liquids—or both?

The Basics Of Matter

This booklet project can be completed at school or at home. Make construction-paper copies of pages 9 and 10 for each student. After each child has cut out his booklet pages and cover, give him three more blank booklet pages. Ask the student to stack his booklet pages so that a blank booklet page follows each duplicated page; then have him place his cover on top of the stack before stapling the booklet together. To complete the booklet, the student cuts pictures that represent the states of matter from discarded magazines, newspapers, and catalogs. He then glues the cutouts on the appropriate booklet pages. Each blank page should be covered with cutouts representing the matter introduced on the previous booklet page. The student also decorates and personalizes the cover of his booklet to his own liking. Students will enjoy looking at their classmates' completed projects. By golly, matter is everywhere!

The Basics Of Matter

by _____

 ## Solids

A solid's a solid.
It doesn't change shape.
It can't move around;
It stays in one place.

Your desk is a solid
And so is your chair.
Just look in your classroom—
Wow! They're everywhere!

Matter Booklet

Use with "The Basics Of Matter" on page 8.

Gases

Air is a gas.
We can't see it, that's true;
But often we feel it
In things that we do.

It keeps up a kite.
Air fills up a bubble.
Without it to breathe,
We would be in BIG trouble.

Liquids

A liquid moves smoothly.
We say that it flows
From one place to another—
How quickly it goes!

We know that most liquids
Are easy to see.
With no shape of their own,
They're not like you and me.

Names_____

Matter In A Bag

Place your marker in the first box.
Follow the directions. Use your bag of matter.

1.
Does your matter take up space?

Yes—go to box 12.
No—go to box 8.

2.
Lay down your bag. Gently press your hand on the bag. Can you make your matter fill the whole bag?
Yes—go to box 6.
No—go to box 5.

3.
Gently squeeze your matter. Can you change the shape of your matter with a squeeze?

Yes—go to box 2.
No—go to box 7.

4.
Are you sure? When you fold down the top of your bag, the size of your matter changes from  to ⬦.
Go back to box 6.
Think about the question again.

5.
Poke your matter with your finger. Does your finger go through the matter?

Yes—go to box 10.
No—go to box 9.

6.
Now try this! Fold down the top of your bag.

Did you change the size of your matter?
Yes—go to box 11.
No—go to box 4.

7.
Squeeze your matter again. Does it change shape?

Yes—go to box 6.
No—go to box 5.

8.
Whoops!
Go back to box 1.
All matter takes up space!

9.
Your matter is a **solid!**

10.
Hold your bag of matter like this:

Now hold it like this:

Did the size of your matter change?

Yes—go to box 15.   **No**—go to box 14.

11.
Your matter is a **gas!**

12.
Place your bag of matter on a balance scale. Does it weigh more than the empty bag?

Yes—go to box 3.
No—go to box 13.

13.
Good try, but you must go back to box 12.

All matter will make the scales tip because all matter has weight.

14.
Your matter is a **liquid!**

15.
Think again! The size of your matter didn't change. Only its shape changed!

Go back to box 10 and choose "No."

Note To Teacher: Use with "Matter In A Bag" on page 7.

SCIENCE IS "SPOOK-TACULAR"

Shadows loom on the ceiling, magic potions bubble, a clap of thunder sounds in the distance, and ghosts fly across the room. Is this a scene from a scary movie? No, it's science class! Captivate your students with these hands-on science experiments and activities that relate to Halloween. Students will have a howling good time!

ideas contributed by Rebecca Olien and Stacie Stone Davis

EXPLORING SHADOWS

Shadows are often used in movies and in television shows to achieve a mysterious effect. Survey students to determine what they believe is going to happen when they see a shadow lurking around a corner in a television show or a movie. Explain that a *shadow* is "the darkness cast when light falls on an opaque object." Then shed some light on the topic of shadows by engaging your students in the activities below.

The Giant Hand

Here's a hands-on shadow activity that your students will enjoy! Divide students into a desired number of small groups and provide each group with a flashlight. In turn have each group member use the flashlight to make a shadow of his hand on his desk. Challenge each student to experiment with the position of the flashlight to increase the size of his shadow so that it covers his desk. Allow each student to explore with the flashlight to make hand shadows on the classroom wall, floor, and/or ceiling. After each student has had a turn, discuss students' observations. Have students describe what happened to the sizes of their shadows when they moved the flashlight closer to, and away from, their hands.

Afterward have each student write a story about a hand shadow that likes to lend a helping hand. Next have each student use a white crayon to trace the outline of his hand on a 9" x 12" sheet of black construction paper, then cut out the hand shape. Mount each student's story, along with his resulting hand "shadow," on a bulletin board titled "Helping Hands."

My Helping Hand
by David

My helping hand goes out on Halloween night. If any little kids drop their Halloween candy, it picks the candy up for them.

Shadow Stories

Have students explore shadows while they're preparing to present a Halloween play. Begin by dividing students into a desired number of small groups. Have each group select a Halloween-related book to present as a play. Or, if desired, challenge each group to write its own Halloween-related story. Then have each group make a list of the characters and important props that need to be included when telling this story. Have each group's members work together to make oaktag characters and props, then tape each oaktag cutout to a ruler or a tongue depressor.

Then, in turn, have each group present its play for classmates. To do this, hold a flashlight so that its light is shining on a bare wall or a piece of poster board. Have each group member hold his oaktag cutout(s) in front of the light (moving the cutout closer to, and away from, the light as desired) in order to act out the play. What a fun and creative way to learn about shadows!

MAGIC POTIONS AND A PALETTE OF PAINTS

Bubble, bubble, toil, and trouble; whip up these "potions" on the double! These bubbling brews and colorful concoctions will help teach students about chemical interactions and color mixing.

Happy Halloween Potion

Making this undrinkable potion will help students see what results when baking soda is added to vinegar. Print the following recipe on a piece of chart paper and then post it in a convenient classroom location:

> **Halloween Potion**
> 1/2 cup lagoon water (vinegar)
> 2 drops dragon blood (red food coloring)
> 1 frog eye (clear marble)
> 5 drops pond scum (green food coloring)
> 1 snake skin (paper shreds)
> 3 pinches of powdered dinosaur bones (baking soda)

Then divide your students into a desired number of small groups. Give each group member a nine-ounce clear plastic cup, a measuring cup, and access to the above ingredients. (Or, if desired, the recipe can be doubled and made in a glass pie pan atop an overhead projector so that all students can see it.) To make the potion, put the first five ingredients together in the cup. Then add the pinches of baking soda. Afterward discuss students' observations about the baking soda being added to the mixture. Guide students to understand that they witnessed a *chemical reaction* between vinegar and baking soda that resulted in carbon dioxide. Explain that *carbon dioxide* is a "tasteless, colorless, and odorless gas exhaled by humans and used in soft drinks to give them their fizz."

Have students discard this mixture and rinse their cups. Then provide students with additional materials—such as other colors of food coloring, coffee grounds, and Styrofoam® packing peanuts—that students can use to create new recipes for vinegar–baking soda potions. Have students write their new recipes on large index cards; then bind them into a book called "Our Halloween Potions."

Fiendish Fizz

After making the Happy Halloween Potion, try making this drinkable treat. For each student, put a small scoop of lime sherbet in the bottom of a nine-ounce clear plastic cup. Pour 1/2 teaspoon of lemon juice over the sherbet; then sprinkle a pinch of baking soda atop the sherbet. Pour lemon-lime soda over the sherbet and then watch the fizz. Drink and enjoy!

> Kevin's Recipe For
> Happy Halloween Potion
> 1 pinch crumbled mouse whiskers (coffee grounds)
> 1/2 cup moat water (vinegar)
> 1 drop algae (green food coloring)
> 1 drop nectar (yellow food coloring)
> 1 ghost tooth (Styrofoam® packing peanut)
> 3 pinches termite dust (baking soda)

Face Paint

Mix up some fun with this color experiment that results in safe-to-wear face paints. To begin, give each child a paper-plate palette on which you have placed six half-tablespoons of vegetable shortening. Each child will also need access to vials of food coloring. Have each child put two drops of red food coloring on one vegetable-shortening blob, then mix it with a wooden coffee stirrer or craft stick. Repeat this process with the yellow and then the blue food coloring, asking students to describe their observations after each mixing session. Then ask students what colors of food coloring could be blended together into the vegetable shortening to create other face-paint colors. List students' responses on the board; then have students use drops of food coloring to test their hypotheses. After a predetermined amount of time, ask students to tell the results of their experiments.

When the face paint–mixing session is complete, have students apply dabs of face paints to create silly faces. Emphasize that the face paints can be washed off easily with soap and warm water, but that they should not be applied near the eyes or nose. As an alternative, have each student decorate a nine-inch paper plate with the face paints.

M-O-O-A-A-N-N-N

GROAN   CLANK CLANK   C-R-E-E-A-A-K

ALL SORTS OF SOUNDS

Creaking doors, rattling chains, a whistling wind, and plenty of moans and groans are all sounds associated with Halloween. Explain that every sound is produced by the vibration of an object. (When the object vibrates, the air around the object vibrates. These vibrations travel in all directions, and when they reach the ears, the brain interprets the vibrations as sounds.) Then have your students explore sound while engaging in these activities.

Spooky Sounds

To introduce this lesson, show students a short video-tape of a cartoon or another Halloween-related show. Ask the students to listen carefully for sound effects, such as the clip-clop of a running horse or the rumble of thunder. Afterward ask students to name the sounds they heard; then write their responses on the board. Explain that sound effects are often created in a studio by people who are using many different materials. (For example, the clip-clop sound of a running horse may be two wooden blocks being tapped on a tabletop.)

Then challenge your students to use materials to create sound effects of their own. Divide students into a desired number of small groups. Invite students to use paper-towel tubes, waxed paper, sheets of tagboard, metal hangers, paper cups, rice, wooden blocks, aluminum foil, pasta, dried leaves, plastic containers, pieces of fabric, and other classroom objects to make sound effects. After a predetermined amount of exploration time, ask each group to demonstrate the sound effects that it created. On a sheet of chart paper, list all of these sound effects.

Our Sound Effects	
Sounds	How We Made The Sounds
rain	dropping rice on foil
opening a present	crumpling waxed paper
people walking	tapping wooden blocks on the desk
thunder	shaking the poster board

clop clop

wiggle wiggle

Sound-Effects Tape

After students have had a chance to explore different sound effects, enlist their help in making a sound-effects tape to complement a Halloween story. Select a story that requires a number of sound effects such as *The Little Old Lady Who Was Not Afraid Of Anything* by Linda Williams (The Trumpet Club, 1990). After reading the book aloud, enlist students' help in naming instances in the story when a sound effect could be inserted, and list their ideas on the board. For each sound effect needed, ask a group of student volunteers to be responsible for making that sound. Give assistance to any group that is not sure how to make its sound. Then, as you read the story aloud again, have each group make its sound effect at the designated time. After you have practiced this one or two times, insert a tape in a tape recorder and record the story with all of the sound effects. If desired, put the tape in a resealable plastic bag and let each student take the tape home to share with his family.

FLYING GHOSTS

For a "spook-tacular" Halloween experiment, make these air-powered ghosts. Pair the students; then give each pair a white balloon. Have one partner inflate the balloon, then hold the end of the balloon while the other partner securely twists a pipe cleaner around the balloon's end. Next give each pair one-half of a plastic drinking straw and some adhesive tape. Have students tape the straw to the side of the balloon as shown. To complete the ghost, each student pair uses a permanent felt-tip marker to add facial features, then tapes four 12-inch crepe-paper lengths to their balloon.

Next have each student pair position their chairs about ten feet apart and directly across from one another. Give each pair a 12-foot length of fishing line. Ask one partner to tape one end of the fishing line to his chair. Ask the other partner to thread the untaped end of the fishing line through the straw so that the top of the balloon ghost is nearer the taped end of the fishing line, then sit in his chair and securely hold the fishing line.

To make the balloon ghost "fly," the partner who is not holding the fishing line untwists the pipe cleaner to release the air from the balloon ghost. The releasing of the air will cause the balloon to move. Afterward have one partner use a yardstick or tape measure to determine the distance of the ghost's flight, then write that distance on a copy of the reproducible below (Trial #1). Have the other partner reinflate the balloon. Then have the pair repeat the process. (Be sure to have extra balloons on hand in case one breaks.) Each time the process is repeated, challenge each student pair to change variables on the balloon ghost (such as the length of the straw piece, the length and/or number of crepe-paper streamers, the tautness of the fishing line, and the amount of air in the balloon) in order to achieve the longest ghost flight possible. For each flight, have one partner record the variables that have been changed, and have the other partner measure and record the distance of the ghost's flight.

Experiment Record Sheet

_____'s and _____'s Flying Ghost

Trial #	Variables Changed	Distance Traveled
1	None changed	
2		
3		
4		
5		

Getting To Know
BATS

Gentle, Fascinating, And Valuable

All over the world people are changing their ideas about bats. Once bats were feared and innocently killed, but now people are learning that bats are harmless, gentle, and very valuable to our environment. Begin to unravel the mystery of the world's most amazing and misunderstood mammal with this collection of enlightening activities. You'll be glad you did; there's no doubt "a-bat" it!

What's Your "Bat-itude"?

Survey your youngsters' attitudes about bats before beginning your bat study. Find out how many youngsters fear bats, have seen bats, or have heard stories about bats that they would like to share. Next have each youngster draw a picture and write a sentence that best describes his feelings about bats on a half-sheet of paper. If desired, collect and store the papers for use at the end of your bat study with "We've Flipped Over Bats!" on page 18.

Explain to students that people often confuse real bats with their make-believe counterparts. Make sure that students understand that the bats they see pictured and portrayed around Halloween are not the real thing!

Billions Of Bats

Trying to learn the names and characteristics of all the bats in the world could drive you absolutely batty! Bats make up nearly a quarter of all the mammals on earth. There are two main groups of bats and about 1,000 different species. To help young students better understand the magnitude of 1,000 different kinds of bats, challenge them as a group to collect 1,000 clean aluminum cans. Bag the cans in groups of 100; then transport them to a local recycling facility. You'll be helping the environment—something bats do every day of their lives!

Nocturnal Nametags

Youngsters are sure to go batty over these bat-shaped nametags. One can only guess what these nocturnal projects do when everyone has gone home for the day! To make a nametag, fold a 9" x 12" sheet of construction paper in half and trace the nametag pattern (page 20) onto the folded paper. Cut on the resulting outlines—not on the fold. Personalize and decorate both sides of the cutout. To complete the project, fold the tabs inward and glue one tab atop the other. When the glue is dry, adjust the folds as needed so that the resulting nametag is freestanding. Tape each student's nametag to his desk. See "The Bat 'Fact-ory' " on page 17 for a related project.

Jolene Pennington—Gr. 1–2, Hutton School,
Chanute, KS

Meet The Micros

Microbats is the larger of the two bat groups. Most of the 800 bat species in this group are small, insect-eating bats that live all over the world. The eyes of microbats are small, but they can probably see as well as mice. Microbats often have large ears and unusual-looking noses that make them unattractive. However these features are an important part of the *echolocation* process which enables them to successfully prey on nocturnal flying insects.

Discuss the benefits of using bats rather than chemical insecticides to control insects. Emphasize that bats are an effective and environmentally safe means of insect control, while chemical insecticides are known to be harmful to man and his environment. For a fun cooperative group activity, have each small group create a pest control company that uses bats instead of insecticides. Have students name their companies and design logos, business cards, company trucks, employee uniforms, and advertisements for the local newspaper or radio station. Encourage each group to stress the environmental benefits that its company provides.

Meet The Megas

This smaller bat group, called *megabats (or flying foxes),* contains the larger bats. These large, fruit-eating bats, which resemble foxes, have large eyes and see quite well. In fact most of them do not use echolocation. These furry bats live mostly in the tropics of Asia and Africa. Unlike microbats, some megabats are active during the day.

Megabats are very important to agriculture and forestry, but their work in dispersing seeds and pollinating plants is often overlooked. Instead fruit growers complain that the bats destroy their crops. Scientists, however, have proven that these bats do not eat unripe fruit. And since most fruit growers harvest their fruit before it has ripened, it is unlikely that these bats pose a threat. More likely they are performing yet another service for the growers. By eating the ripe fruit that remains after the harvest, bats are reducing the breeding grounds and food supply of the harmful fruit fly.

To make a tasty point about the helpfulness of the fruit-eating bats, make a Fruit Bat Salad. Ask students to bring from home a variety of fruits associated with bats such as bananas, mangoes, dates, figs, avocados, and papayas. Cut up and mix the fruits together for a tasty treat. Thank you, bats!

There's No Place Like Home

Bats live in all sorts of places around the world. In fact, the only continent that bats do not inhabit is Antarctica. A bat's home or *roost* can be in a variety of places. Some bats live in caves, some live in treetops, and others live deep in hollow logs. In India there are even bats that live underground with porcupines! Many other bat roosts are in the nooks and crannies of castles, churches, and homes. Amazingly enough, one bat may have a dozen or more roosts.

Ask youngsters how they might feel if bats moved into their homes. Explain that once people in Europe thought that it was unlucky for bats to enter their homes, while people in China welcomed the visitors because they supposedly brought good luck. For a fun creative-writing project, have students write and illustrate stories about bats that move into their homes. Encourage students to write about where the bats made their roosts, how their families liked the batty visitors, and what kinds of luck (if any) the bats brought with them. Be sure to provide time for students to share their creative tales.

The Bat "Fact-ory"

To entice further interest in bats, display this sampling of amazing bat facts. After reading and discussing each one, have students copy the facts onto individual 1 1/2" x 9" construction-paper slips. For nifty storage, have students slip the fact strips inside their bat-shaped nametags. (See "Nocturnal Nametags" on page 16.) Keep a supply of colorful construction-paper strips and a variety of bat-related resources on hand so that students can add to their bat fact collections. Each day invite students to share any new bat facts they have discovered. At the end of the project, help each youngster bind his fact strips together using a brad of the appropriate size. Now that's a handy reference of batty facts!

Amazing But True
- One type of bat scoops fish out of water.
- Fruit-eating bats help spread tree seeds in rain forests.
- Bat waste is called *guano* and is a valuable fertilizer.
- Bats are a tourist attraction in Austin, Texas.
- The smallest mammal on earth is the bumblebee bat of Thailand. It weighs less than one penny.

Bat Conservation International

For bats, conservation cannot begin without education, which is a major focus of Bat Conservation International. For information about bat-related teaching materials, call 1-800-538-BATS or write to:

**Bat Conservation International
Educators' Packet**
P.O. Box 162603
Austin, TX 78716-2603

Brushing Up On Bats

Is that a fact? Give youngsters an opportunity to showcase their fact and opinion skills with this center activity. Duplicate a supply of the open game cards on page 24. Divide students into small groups, and instruct each group to program fact and opinion cards for the center. Later mount selected cards on construction paper, program a corresponding answer key, and create a gameboard similar to the one shown.

Store the cards and answer key inside an envelope. A student removes the contents of the envelope and sets the answer key aside (facedown) before he reads and sorts the cards on top of the gameboard. Then he uses the answer key to check his work.

adapted from an idea by Kathleen Knoblock, Torrance, CA

We've Flipped Over Bats!

For an eye-opening culminating activity, have students repeat the activity described in "What's Your 'Bat-itude'?" on page 16. This time, instead of collecting the papers, redistribute the youngsters' work from the first activity. Invite students to share how their feelings about bats have changed (if appropriate).

For added fun, have each student prepare his project for display at a bulletin board entitled "We've Flipped Over Bats!" To prepare a project, fold in half a colorful sheet of 9" x 12" construction paper and mount one paper to each side of the folded paper. (The lower edge of each paper should be positioned near the fold.) Using a tagboard tracer of the pattern on page 20, trace and cut out a bat shape from a 6" x 9" sheet of construction paper. Decorate both sides of the cutout; then position and glue or staple the tab between the open ends of the folded project. Use lengths of yarn to suspend the projects from pushpins inserted into the bulletin board. "Battacular"!

A Real Batman

Merlin D. Tuttle has rightly earned the title of "batman." Founder of Bat Conservation International, Dr. Tuttle has led the drive to reeducate people with the truth about bats. Tuttle's fascination with bats began almost by accident. Although he was interested in nature at an early age, it was not until he was in high school that bats piqued his curiosity. In fact if his family had not moved to Knoxville, Tennessee, about two miles from a bat cave, Tuttle may not have been so intrigued by these strange creatures. *Batman: Exploring The World Of Bats* (page 19) gives a captivating account of Tuttle's life and accomplishments, as well as a wealth of amazing bat information.

Have youngsters support Tuttle's efforts and spread the real facts about bats. Duplicate student copies of the badge pattern on page 20. To make the badges, have students color and cut out the badge patterns, then glue them atop slightly larger construction-paper circles. To wear the badges, have each student use a hole punch to punch a hole near the top of his badge, then thread a length of yarn through the hole and tie the yarn ends. Or use a safety pin to attach the badge to each youngster's clothing.

BATTY
About Books!

Enhance your study of bats with this collection of entertaining and informative books.

Stellaluna
Written & Illustrated by Janell Cannon
Published by Harcourt Brace Jovanovich, Publishers

If your youngsters haven't yet developed a soft spot for bats, this endearing tale will do the trick! One evening Stellaluna, a baby fruit bat, is knocked from the clutches of her mother by a hungry owl. Too young to have mastered the art of flying, the baby bat tumbles downward and eventually plunges headfirst into a nest with three startled baby birds. What follows are Stellaluna's attempts to adapt to the habits of her new family. The result is a sweet, enlightening, and at times humorous story of friendship and understanding that is just too good to miss!

Loose Tooth
Written by Steven Kroll & Illustrated by Tricia Tusa
Published by Holiday House, Inc.

This batty book is sure to be favored by your youngsters. Flapper and Fangs are twin bats who share everything and do almost everything together. But when Fangs gets a loose tooth, the twosome has some troubles. Flapper feels terribly ignored—so ignored that he decides to pull a batty stunt to foil the tooth fairy's visit. But the stunt doesn't quite turn out as expected!

A First Look At Bats
Written by Millicent E. Selsam and Joyce Hunt & Illustrated by Harriett Springer
Published by Walker And Company

One in a series of nature books written for children, this selection is packed with valuable information about the world's only flying mammal. Popular myths are dispelled and interesting facts are provided. Unique in its format, the book also presents several different bat species and asks its young readers to compare and contrast the bats' physical characteristics. A perfect choice for beginning bat fans.

Eyewitness Juniors: Amazing Bats
Written by Frank Greenaway & Photographed by Jerry Young and Frank Greenaway
Published by Alfred A. Knopf, Inc.

As its title suggests, this book features a collection of amazing facts about bats. Each two-page spread contains a large photograph of a bat accompanied by brief text containing fascinating facts. Share the pictures and read and discuss some of the facts to further pique your youngsters' interest in these furry creatures.

Shadows Of Night: The Hidden World Of The Little Brown Bat
Written & Illustrated by Barbara Bash
Published by Sierra Club Books

At the opening of this beautifully illustrated book, a pregnant bat joins a maternity colony after a two-night, hundred-mile flight from her winter hibernation cave. Soon after, the baby bat is born, and the lives of the new mother and her baby unfold. Students are sure to be captivated by this intriguing look at bat life.

Batman: Exploring The World Of Bats
Written by Laurence Pringle & Photographed by Merlin D. Tuttle
Published by Charles Scribner's Sons Books For Young Readers

Introduce students to a dedicated scientist whose initiative, research, and perseverance have earned him the title of "batman." In this very readable biography, students learn about the childhood and dreams of Merlin D. Tuttle (batman) and the impact he has had and still has on the bat world today.

Patterns

Use with "A Real Batman" on page 18.

I'm
BATTY
about bats!

Please ask me about them!

Place on fold.

Place on fold.

Use with
"Nocturnal Nametags"
on page 16.

tab

Also use with
"We've Flipped Over
Bats!" on page 18.
(For this project,
disregard the
programming on
the pattern.)

©1997 The Education Center, Inc. • *The Best Of* The Mailbox® *Science • Primary* • TEC836

A Pocketful Of Science

Bats And Sound

Bats are equipped in remarkable ways to hunt at night. They use sound waves and a technique called *echolocation.* Using these activities, you can further explore the uniqueness of these nocturnal creatures and introduce the basic principles of sound.　*ideas by Ann Flagg*

Activity 1: Vibrations

You will need:
one large rubber band per student

What to do:
Have youngsters firmly grasp one end of their rubber bands in each hand, then release their index fingers and thumbs. Then, using their thumbs and index fingers, have students pluck and strum their rubber bands to make a variety of sounds. Instruct students to carefully watch their rubber bands as they listen to the sounds being made.

Questions to ask:
1. Were all of the sounds you made alike?
2. What was the rubber band doing when you heard a sound?

Next:
Have each child place his fingers on the bony part of his throat; then lead students in a chorus of sounds. For example say, "Ahhhhhh," "Eeeeeee," and "Mmmmmmm." Have each student describe to a classmate what he felt with his fingers. Then have each child invent a sound of his own and describe what he felt.

Questions to ask:
1. What did you feel when you said, "Ahhhhhh," and touched your throat?
2. Did all of the sounds you made feel the same to your fingers?
3. Think about the rubber band. What do you think might be happening inside your throat when you talk, sing, or make other sounds?

This is why:

Sound is given off when something vibrates. A person's vocal cords vibrate like rubber bands across a voice box. When you touch the bony part of your throat (the Adam's apple) and make a sound, you can feel the vibrations of the vocal cords.

Activity 2: Sound Waves

You will need:
glass pan or clear plastic container filled with one inch of water
food coloring (optional)
eyedropper full of water
overhead projector

What to do:
If desired, use the food coloring to tint the water. Place the pan of water on the overhead projector and project the watery image. When the water becomes calm, use the eyedropper to drop a droplet of water into the pan. Repeat this procedure.

Questions to ask:
1. What did you see when each water droplet fell into the pan of water?
2. What happened when the water waves reached the sides of the pan?

This is why:

Although we cannot see sound waves, the circular waves that were seen in the water are similar to how sound waves travel through the air. When the water waves bounced off the sides of the pan and moved back towards the middle, you saw how an echo is formed. (When you hear an echo, your sound waves have hit and bounced off a very hard surface, and then traveled back to you!)

Pam Crane

Activity 3: Extraordinary Hearing

You will need:
a selection of music and a method of playing it
student copies of page 23

What to do:
Distribute the student activity pages and ask youngsters to study the bats pictured. Explain that bats are amazing nighttime hunters; then ask students to brainstorm reasons why this might be so. Next play the music and ask students to listen carefully. Keep the music volume low. After several seconds, turn the music off. Have youngsters cup their hands and place one cupped hand behind each of their ears. Keeping their hands cupped, have students gently extend each ear, bringing their outer ears forward. In this position, have students listen to the same selection of music again.

Questions to ask:
1. Did you notice a difference in the music when you listened to it the second time? If so, what was the difference?
2. Why do you think the music sounded louder?
3. How might a bat's large ears help make it a better hunter?

This is why:

Sound travels through the air in waves, which spread out in all directions (see Activity 2). When students listened to the music the first time, a few sound waves reached their ears, but most of the waves bypassed their ears and traveled across the room. When the students' ears were cupped, more sound waves were captured and channeled to their ears. This made the music sound louder. Bats' ears are large and cupped, therefore much more efficient than human ears. Bats can hear and capture a tiny mosquito in complete darkness! In fact, using echolocation (see Activity 4), a bat can catch as many as 600 mosquitoes in one hour!

Next:
Have each student complete his activity sheet by drawing and illustrating a bat as described.

Activity 4: Echolocation

You will need:
a blindfold

What to do:
Use this large-group game to simulate echolocation. To introduce the game, explain that bats use sound waves, echoes, and their amazing ears to catch tiny insects and moths at night. Then have students form a large circle in an open area. Blindfold one child (the bat) and lead her to the center of the circle. Appoint several other youngsters to be moths and ask them to step inside the circle. Have the remaining students evenly space themselves around the circle and act as trees. To play, the bat and the moths carefully move around inside the circle. The bat repeatedly calls out in a high squeaky voice, "Moth?" and the moths, using loud voices, repeatedly answer, "Moth!" The object of the game is for the bat to listen carefully and tag as many moths as possible within an allotted amount of time. When a moth is tagged, she becomes a tree. If the bat wanders too close to the edge of the circle, the trees nearby whisper, "Tree! Tree!" and carefully help steer the bat back on course. (Whispering keeps the trees from overpowering the moths.) Play as many rounds of the game as desired.

Questions to ask:
1. Why must the bat call out?
2. Why must the moths respond each time the bat calls out?

This is why:

Bats make rapid squeaking sounds that are usually too high-pitched for human ears to hear. If an insect is flying near a bat, these sounds bounce off the insect and echoes are heard by the bat. (In the game the moths' responses simulated these echoes.) The resulting echoes inform the bat how far away the insect is, as well as the shape and size of the insect. This is called echolocation. Bats avoid trees and other obstacles in the same manner. Because echolocation is so important to bats, they are constantly flying around with their mouths open making squeaking noises. Since people cannot hear the sounds, they often mistake a bat's open mouth as a sign of aggression, when in fact it is only navigating.

Name_____

The Incredible Bat

Bats are excellent nighttime hunters.
Look at each bat face below.

1.
Caribbean White Bat

2.
Spear-Nosed Bat

3.
Slit-Faced Bat

Remember how a bat hunts.
Draw and color a new kind of bat that will be a great hunter.
Write its name on the line.

_____

Note To Teacher: Use this activity with "Activity 3: Extraordinary Hearing" on page 22.

Open Game Cards
Use with "Brushing Up On Bats" on page 18.

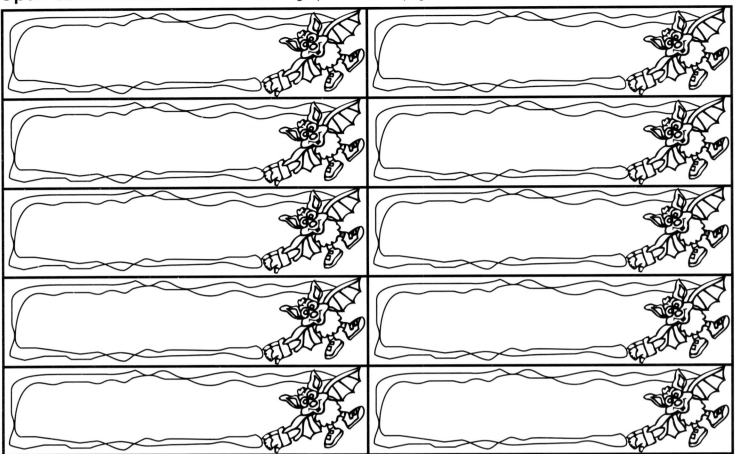

Awards
Duplicate and present the awards to students as desired.

Hi, _____!
I just swooped by to say:

_____
_____
_____

From: _____

©1997 The Education Center, Inc.

Now Hear This!

_____
knows the facts about **BATS**!

Signed _____

Date _____
©1997 The Education Center, Inc.

©1997 The Education Center, Inc. • *The Best Of* The Mailbox® *Science* • *Primary* • TEC836

A Pocketful Of Science

Moon Talk

Use these hands-on activities to introduce facts about the moon.

ideas by Ann Flagg

Activity 1: Sizing Up The Moon

For each student, you will need:

one small index card   scissors

What to do:

Ask students to close their eyes and imagine the moon and a star in their minds. While the youngsters' eyes are closed, have a show of hands to find out how many students "see" the moon as the larger of the two objects. Then ask students to open their eyes. Explain that the following activity will help them understand why the moon looks larger than the stars in the sky when, in fact, the moon is much smaller than the stars we see.

To begin, have each child fold his index card in half; then starting at the fold, have him cut a large rectangle from the center of the folded card. Next have students unfold their cards and carry the resulting *frames* outside onto the playground. As a safety measure, pair students and designate a *scientist* and a *spotter* in each pair. Have each scientist close one eye and use his open eye to look at the playground area through his frame. Ask the scientists to zero in on a playground object. (The entire object must be seen through the frame.) Then have the scientists move slowly toward the objects. (Instruct the spotters to warn the scientists of obstacles in their path and to prevent collisions between students.) Periodically ask the scientists to stop and explain what is happening to the objects they're viewing. When a scientist reaches his object, he and his partner switch roles and repeat the activity. Return to the classroom when all students have participated as scientists and spotters.

Questions to ask:

1. What happened to the object inside your frame as you walked toward it?
2. Why do you think the object seemed to grow as you approached it?
3. How does this activity help you understand why the moon looks larger than the stars, when it really isn't?

This is why:

Children often consider the moon to be larger than the stars they see and about the same size as the sun. The moon has this appearance because it is earth's closest neighbor. If the moon and the sun were placed side by side, the moon would be about 400 times smaller than the sun, which is a medium-sized star!

Activity 2: On The Move

You will need:

a handheld poster labeled for each of the following:
"Earth," "Moon," "Sun"

an open area such as the school gym or playground

What to do:

Gather students in the open area. Select one child to hold the "Sun" sign. As you position the sun in the center of the open area, facing her classmates, explain that *the sun is the center of our solar system.* Select another child to hold the "Earth" sign. As you position the earth about two yards away from the sun, explain that *the earth revolves (or moves) around the sun.* Then set the earth in motion by asking her to maintain her distance from the sun as she slowly walks around it. Choose another child to hold the "Moon" sign. Explain that *the moon revolves around the earth.* Then help the moon slide into place and begin walking around the earth as the earth revolves around the sun. As soon as the earth has completed one revolution around the sun, enlist three different children to recreate the solar scenario. If time permits, allow each youngster a chance to participate in the reenactment.

Once students understand the relationships between these three celestial bodies, explain that both the earth and the moon spin like tops as they revolve around the sun. The sun also spins and is constantly revolving around the center of the Milky Way galaxy. Older students may wish to incorporate these spins into their demonstrations.

Questions to ask:

1. Why do you think the sun is called the center of our solar system?
2. How is the moon's orbit different from the earth's?

This is why:

The sun is considered the center of our solar system because the earth and the other eight planets in our solar system travel around it. The earth travels around the sun approximately once every 365 1/4 days. The moon travels around the earth approximately once every 29 1/2 days with reference to the sun, making the moon's orbit much shorter than the earth's.

Follow-up:

Give each student two brads and a construction-paper copy of page 27. Then, following the directions on the page, have each student color and cut out the sun, moon, and earth pieces and assemble the project as described. Provide assistance as needed.

Pam Crane

Activity 3: Misunderstood Moonlight

You will need:

sunlight   a hand mirror   a powerful flashlight

What to do:

While your students are out of the classroom, set up a mirror so that it catches the sun and reflects a bright spot of light onto a conspicuous classroom location. When the students return and notice the reflection, ask them what could be causing the bright spot of light. After a bit of discussion, direct their attention to the mirror. Find out how many students think the mirror is the source of the light. Next move the mirror out of the sun's path and turn off the lights in the room. After the students have noted that the mirror makes no light, shine the flashlight onto the mirror. Guide students to conclude that the mirror makes no light of its own; however light can bounce off (or *reflect* from) the mirror, causing it to shine.

Questions to ask:

1. In this demonstration, what do you think represents the moon?
2. If the moon has no light of its own, why does it appear to shine and glow at night?
3. What do you think shines on the moon?

This is why:

Like the mirror, the moon makes no light of its own—it is not a luminous body. The moon shines by reflecting sunlight. Like the earth, half of the moon is always lighted by the sun's direct rays, and the other half is always in shadow. The moon has phases because as the moon travels around the earth, different parts of its bright side are seen from the earth. Without the sun, there would be no moonlight.

Activity 4: Countless Craters

In advance: (For the best results, plan this activity around the time of a full moon.)

To begin, ask each youngster to draw and color a full moon from memory on a sheet of drawing paper. After each student has personalized his work and labeled it "Memory Moon," collect the drawings. Next have each child personalize a second sheet of paper and label it "Moon Observation." Have students take these papers home. Ask students to observe the moon that evening, draw and color exactly what they see on their papers, and return the illustrations to school the following school day.

For each student, you will need:

a widemouthed plastic cup half-filled with flour, cornstarch, or baking soda   one marble
      "Memory Moon" drawing
      "Moon Observation" drawing

What to do:

Ask students to compare and contrast their two moon drawings. Most likely a few of the observation drawings will include gray patches or black spots on the moon's surface. Direct students' attention to these patches and ask them to speculate what they might be. After some discussion, explain that the moon's surface contains broad flat plains, rough mountainous highlands, and billions of craters (the most numerous feature). When viewed with an unaided eye, these features appear as dark patches. Further explain that the craters are formed when solid objects hurl through space and crash into the moon.

To demonstrate how craters are formed, disburse the cup and marble supplies listed above. Have each student tap his cup atop his desk to level its contents, then hold his marble over the cup so that the marble is even with the cup rim. On your signal, have all students release the marbles into their cups. Ask students to examine the resulting craters; then have each student carefully remove his marble and level the contents of his cup before repeating the procedure—this time dropping the marble into the cup from several inches above the cup rim.

Questions to ask:

1. How did the size of the first crater compare to the size of the second crater? Why?
2. Do you think a heavier marble would make a bigger crater? Why or why not?

This is why:

The solar system is filled with solid objects—meteoroids—that travel through space. Unlike the earth, the moon does not have a protective shield or atmosphere that helps to slow down, melt, or break apart these hurling objects. Most of the small craters on the moon were formed by the impacts of meteoroids crashing into the moon's surface. The larger craters were probably formed by larger celestial bodies (like asteroids and comets) hitting the moon's surface. The largest crater on the moon—the Imbrium Basin—is 700 miles wide!

Literature Connection

Noted astronomer Dr. E. C. Krupp introduces young readers to our nearest celestial neighbor in *The Moon And You* (published by Macmillan Publishing Company). This outstanding resource book includes fascinating, up-to-date information on gravity, tides, the moon's phases, and moon mythology.

Name _____

Out-Of-This-World Orbits!

Sample:

Color the earth, the moon, and the sun.

Cut out the patterns.

Punch a hole in each strip at the ▲ and the ◉ .

Push a brad through the ◉ in the center of the earth pattern and through the hole in the moon's strip. Open the brad.

Push a brad through the ▲ in the center of the sun pattern and through the hole in the earth's strip. Open the brad.

Show the orbits of the moon and the earth by moving the patterns as shown.

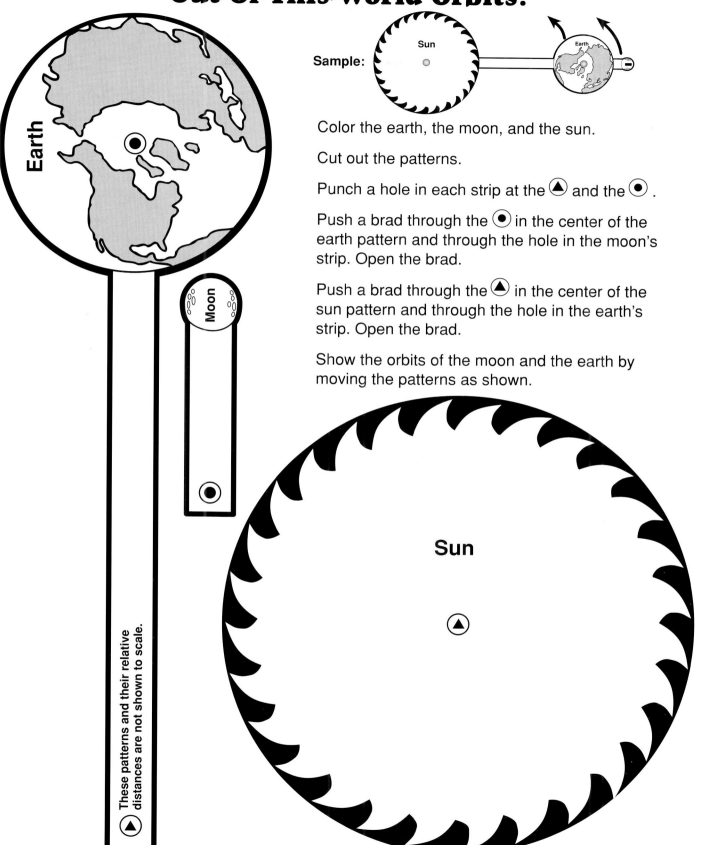

These patterns and their relative distances are not shown to scale.

Note To Teacher: Use this activity after completing "Activity 2: On The Move" on page 25. Each student needs two brads, crayons, and scissors, and access to a hole puncher.

HANGING Out With Spiders

Spiders come in many shapes and sizes, and live just about anywhere they can find food. In fact, a dozen or more different spider varieties could be living in and around your school! But don't fret—spiders are among the most helpful arachnids known to people. Use the following activities to weave a web of intriguing spider lore. Hanging out with these eight-legged wonders is anything but creepy!

by Christine A. Thuman

Overcoming Arachnophobia

Remember Little Miss Muffet? As a class recite this familiar nursery rhyme. Then find out how many students would feel frightened if a spider sat down beside them! Explain that people who have a fear of spiders have *arachnophobia*. Take a poll to find out how many students think Miss Muffet suffered from arachnophobia. Then ask students to give reasons why people fear spiders. List these reasons on a chart entitled "Are You Arachnophobic?" In conclusion, emphasize that the spider is one of nature's most useful and extraordinary creatures. Thanks to spiders, a tremendous number of insects that would otherwise harm our environment, are eaten.

An Itty-Bitty Spider Ditty

Reinforce the positive aspects of the arachnid family with this upbeat spider song!

Spider, Spider

(sung to the tune of "Daisy, Daisy")

Spider, Spider, you are a friend, I know.
You eat bugs that eat little plants that grow.
You really are not so scary. You're not so very hairy.
You have eight feet. Your web is neat. Little spidery friend
of mine.

Lucia Kemp Henry, Fallon, NV

Getting The Facts

Once students begin learning the facts about spiders, their aversion to the eight-legged critters can quickly be converted into curiosity. An excellent book to begin with is *Eyewitness Juniors Amazing Spiders* by Alexandra Parsons. In this book, each two-page spread contains a large picture of a spider surrounded by brief text containing fascinating facts. Share the pictures, and read and discuss some of the facts to pique your youngsters' interest.

Finally show the class some harmless live spiders that you've placed in vented containers. Have students observe the body structure and habits of the captured spiders for one day. Then set the spiders free!

What A Body!

All spiders have eight legs attached to the front part of their body, or *cephalothorax*. But did you know that most spiders also have eight eyes? A spider's body is an intricate network of precision parts. To learn more about the spider's amazing body, give each student a copy of the puzzle on page 32 and a 9" x 12" sheet of construction paper. To work the puzzle, a student cuts out his puzzle pieces and arranges them atop his construction paper to form a spider body. After the student glues his puzzle pieces in place, he cuts out the puzzle labels and glues each label in its matching box. When the glue has thoroughly dried, the student can color his spider and personalize his project as desired. Use the following information to lead a discussion that relates to each of the body parts shown on the puzzle:

cephalothorax *(sef•ah•low•THOR•ax):* All eight legs are connected to this front part of the spider's body. This combined head-and-chest area also stores the spider's brain and stomach.

abdomen: This is the rear section of the spider's body. A spider's silk is produced by silk glands located here.

legs: All spiders have four pairs of legs. The legs are covered with hairs that serve as sense organs. They pick up vibrations and smells from the air. All spiders have at least two tiny claws at the end of each leg.

eyes: Most spiders have eight eyes set in two rows. However some species have as few as six, four, two, or no eyes. The majority of spiders do not have good eyesight.

chelicerae *(kuh•LIS•uh•ree):* Sometimes called the jaws of a spider, these structures are found above a spider's mouth. Each has a fang tip that has a poison duct opening near the end.

pedipalps *(PED•eh•palps):* These leglike limbs at the sides of the mouth serve as a spider's "feelers."

spinnerets *(SPIN•uh•rehts):* Usually a spider has six tiny spinnerets, or tubes, at the rear of its abdomen. Silk is released through these openings. Spiders make several kinds of silk. Some silk is sticky, while other kinds are dry. Spider silk is produced as a liquid, but it hardens when it is exposed to air.

Most likely, students will be eager to take another look at your captured spider friends. (See "Getting The Facts.") If possible, provide a few handheld magnifying glasses for this purpose. Be sure to have several spider books on hand so students can research any spider-related questions they might have.

Pam Crane

Expert Weavers

Some spiders create amazing webs with their thin strands of silk. Webs vary in shape and size—from the postage stamp–size web of the dwarf spider to the humongous 30-foot web of the tropical banana spider. The design of a spider's web depends on the spider's species. The beautiful *orb web* of a garden spider can be found around buildings or on school grounds in the early fall. Orb webs are easy to identify because of their spiral patterns. If you can find an orb web within easy reach, take the following steps to capture the web. Many garden spiders build new webs each night, so look for one early in the morning before it has been damaged by insects.

Steps to capture a web:
1. Sprinkle the web with talcum powder.
2. Spray adhesive onto a large sheet of dark-colored construction paper.
3. Carefully flatten the construction paper against the web. (Because the talcum powder clings to the sticky threads of the web, the web can be easily seen against the dark paper.)

Display the captured web in your classroom. After each student has closely inspected the web, challenge students to learn more about how a garden spider spins and uses her web.

Woven With Care

Invite your spider enthusiasts to spin webs of their own! On day one of this two-day painting project, have students paint backgrounds for their webs. To do this, a student uses a wide brush and green, purple, or blue tempera paint to cover a large sheet of art paper. Encourage students to vary the intensity of their background colors as they paint. On day two, have each student use a fine brush and white tempera paint to make a web on her painted background. Students may create orb webs or original web designs. Mount the completed projects on a display entitled "Woven With Care."

For a fun writing extension, have each student write a spider story to accompany her web project. If desired, have students make colorful eight-legged booklets. Students can copy their stories inside their booklets, then dangle them from their webs. What a sight!

Arachnids In Action

If you've ever done any spider watching, you know how talented these creatures can be! From building intricate webs to making clever underground traps and tunnels, spiders conquer their prey. While all spiders are avid hunters, their hunting methods vary from species to species. *Sedentary spiders* (also known as *web weavers*) stay in one place and catch their prey with the aid of elaborate webs. *Wandering spiders* (sometimes referred to as *hunters*) catch their prey by stalking it and pouncing on it. Simulate the differences between these two types of hunting methods with the following games:

Waiting In The Web
Number Of Players: Two teams (Sedentary Spiders & Insects)
Equipment Needed: A large defined area of play, approximately 50 small index cards (food), one 3-foot yarn length for each member of the spider team (webs)
Directions: Randomly distribute the index cards (food) inside the playing area; then ask each member of the spider team to lay his web in a straight line near some food. Spiders stay inside the playing area. They may move up and down their webs, but must keep one foot on their webs at all times. To play, the insects travel back and forth across the playing area trying to gather food without being captured (tagged) by a web-spinning spider. A tagged insect must immediately crouch. Continue play until all (or most) of the food has been gathered or all (or most) of the insects have been captured. Then have the teams switch roles and play the game a second time.

Ready To Pounce
Number Of Players: Two teams (Wandering Spiders & Insects)
Equipment Needed: A large defined area of play, approximately 50 small index cards (food), one soft foam-rubber ball for each member of the spider team (method of surprise)
Directions: Randomly distribute the index cards (food) inside the playing area; then ask each member of the spider team to position himself inside the playing area. Each spider must keep one foot firmly planted. To play, the insects travel back and forth across the playing area trying to gather food. To capture (tag) an insect, a wandering spider tosses his soft foam-rubber ball, trying to hit the insect below the waist. If the insect is hit, it crouches immediately. If it is not, the insect continues to move through the playing area. Either way, the wandering spider moves to where his ball has landed. From his new position he tries to capture another insect. Continue play until all (or most) of the food has been gathered or all (or most) of the insects have been captured. Then have the teams switch roles and play the game a second time.

Eight-Legged Prose

Students are sure to get a kick out of writing "spiderish" poetry! In advance duplicate a class supply of construction-paper spider bodies using the pattern on page 31, and cut a colorful supply (eight-per-child minimum) of 1" x 4 1/2" construction-paper strips. Also display two lengths of bulletin-board paper. Label one paper "Adjectives" and the other "Verbs." Begin the activity by asking students to brainstorm words that describe spiders and their actions. Under your youngsters' direction, list the words on the appropriate posters. When a desired number of words are listed, have each child select eight paper strips. Ask each youngster to choose four adjectives and four verbs from the lists and write each word in the center of a different paper strip.

Then, on a sheet of his own paper, have each youngster draft a poem (any kind will do) that includes all eight of his words. Once the poems are written, pair students and have the partners work together to edit the poems they've written. Later, working individually, have students use fine-tipped markers to copy their edited poems onto the duplicated spider bodies. To complete his spider project, a child cuts out the spider body and attaches the paper-strip legs to the cutout. (See the illustration.) Then, using markers or crayons, he decorates and personalizes his spider to his own liking before creasing the paper strips to resemble spider legs.

Kooky Spiders

Unlike the real thing, these spiders are quite tasty! Conclude your spider studies with this no-bake treat. Before your youngsters indulge in their edible delights, ask them to explain what is anatomically correct and incorrect about their kooky spider cookies. Once the facts are in, eat away!

To make these kooky spiders, you will need one sandwich cookie and four 4-inch strings of licorice per student, white frosting tinted with food coloring, plastic knives for spreading the frosting, and a supply of colorful cake-decorating candies. A student carefully opens his sandwich cookie and centers his licorice strings over the cream filling. He spreads a thin layer of frosting inside the remaining cookie half and presses it atop the licorice strings. Next he spreads a thin layer of frosting on top of the cookie and presses two to eight cake-decorating candies (eyes) into the icing. "Spider-rific"!

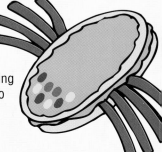

Speaking Out About Spiders

Not even Miss Muffet could run away from these adorable spiders! Without a doubt arachnids will be the talk of the school when your youngsters get these spider brooches assembled and pinned to their clothing. To begin a spider brooch, cut a small circle from a sponge or begin with a circular makeup sponge. Use a narrow strip of sticky tape, such as duct tape, to attach the center of a bundle of four pipe-cleaner lengths to one side of your sponge. Using a second piece of tape, tape the base of a safety pin atop the pipe-cleaner bundle. Spread apart and bend the pipe cleaners to resemble the legs of a spider. Attach a pom-pom to the sponge to complete the spider's body. Use craft glue, glitter, fabric paints, and other supplies to embellish the spider as desired. When the projects are dry, assist students in pinning on the spiders. Encourage students to share spider facts with the folks who comment on their sparkling spider friends.

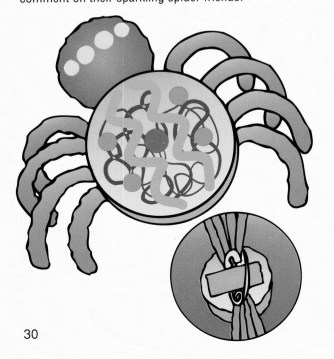

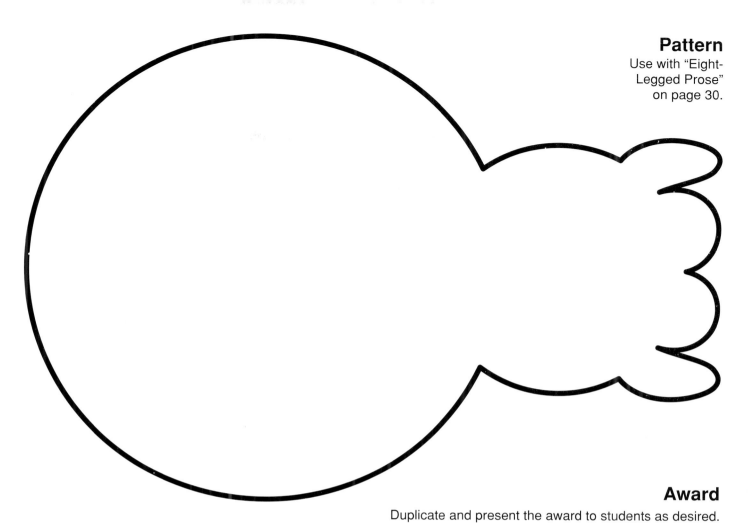

Pattern
Use with "Eight-Legged Prose"
on page 30.

Award
Duplicate and present the award to students as desired.

Please Take Note!

has become a
skillful spinner of
spider facts!

Signed

Date

Spider Puzzle

Use with "What A Body!" on page 28.

Puzzle Pieces

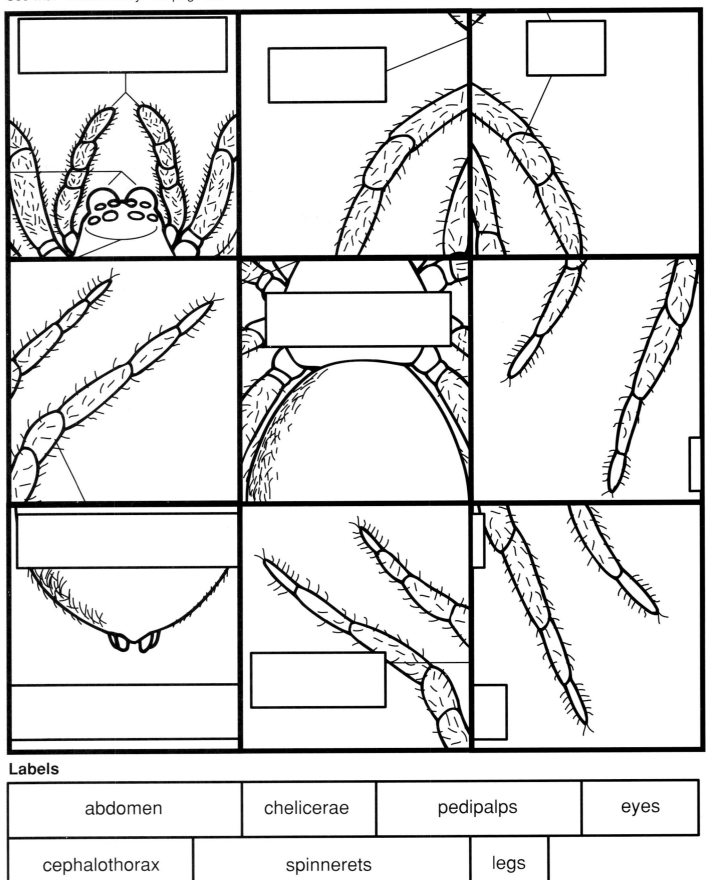

Labels

abdomen	chelicerae	pedipalps	eyes

cephalothorax	spinnerets	legs

MAY THE FORCE BE WITH YOU!

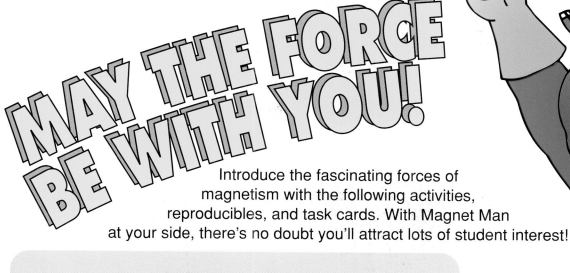

Introduce the fascinating forces of magnetism with the following activities, reproducibles, and task cards. With Magnet Man at your side, there's no doubt you'll attract lots of student interest!

A Mysterious Force

Brainstorm with your students what it must have been like to discover magnetism. How would people explain the strange pulling force? Would people believe their stories? No one knows for certain who first discovered magnetism, though several stories exist. One story tells about a sheepherder named Magnes who noticed that the iron nails in his shoes were attracted to certain rocks. This event is believed to have taken place about 3,000 years ago in the country of Magnesia. Another story tells that in China, nearly 5,000 years ago, certain rocks were discovered to attract pieces of iron.

Have students enlist parent help as they prepare lists of household items that utilize the forces of magnetism. Encourage students to share the items on their lists; then have each student illustrate one item on drawing paper and cut it out. Display the cutouts on a giant horseshoe-shaped magnet cut from bulletin board paper.

The Poles Of A Magnet

Here's an experiment that shows why the ends of a magnet are called the north pole and the south pole. Post signs which identify the directions north and south. Tie one end of a piece of thread around the middle of a bar magnet. Tape the other end of the thread to the underside of a wooden table or chair. (Make certain there are no other magnets or objects made from iron, steel, nickel, or cobalt close by.) Let the magnet dangle. When the magnet stops moving, one end will be pointing north—the north pole of the magnet. The other end will be pointing south—the south pole of the magnet. Challenge students to identify an instrument that always points north (a compass); then guide them to conclude that a compass needle must be a magnet!

Why The Attraction?

Help students better understand the pull of magnetism with this simple demonstration. Tie a stack of three heavy books in the center of a long jump rope. Choose four student volunteers of approximately the same size and strength, and position two of them at each end of the rope. Instruct the volunteers to pull their rope ends until you signal them to stop (in just a few seconds). Next retie the books at one end of the jump rope, position all four volunteers at the opposite end of the rope, and instruct them to carefully pull the rope. Discuss the outcomes of the two demonstrations. Point out that there are tiny moving bits inside all objects (molecules). If the tiny bits are not working together (like the first demonstration) they do not create a strong force. But when the tiny bits work together (like the second demonstration) they create a strong force called magnetism.

Losing The Force

Reinforce the importance of proper magnet care with this activity. Provide each student with nine 1" x 2" pieces of white construction paper and a 3" x 6" piece of construction paper. Fold each of the smaller rectangles in half, then color the halves red and yellow as shown. Color the reverse sides to match. Position the smaller rectangles atop the larger rectangle to portray the molecules of a magnet. Discuss the importance of the molecules' positions in creating a magnetic force. Have students predict what will happen when they drop their "paper magnets" on the floor, and if this procedure will affect their magnets' magnetism. Next instruct students to slide their paper magnets to the floor. After students have collected the scattered molecules, explain that the molecules in a real magnet can be rearranged if it is dropped, hit hard, or left in a very hot place. When a magnet's molecules are out of line, the magnet loses its magnetic force.

"Attractive" Pictures

This art activity illustrates the magnetic fields of magnets. At a table, provide two or three magnets, a container of iron filings (may be obtained from a machine shop or by cutting steel wool into tiny pieces with an old pair of scissors), a plastic spoon, large plain index cards, and hair spray or clear, plastic fixative spray. With adult supervision, a student lays an index card atop the magnets. He then uses the plastic spoon to sprinkle iron filings on top of the card. The filings will collect in patterns illustrating the magnetic fields of the magnets. The adult then sprays the card with the spray fixative provided. Respray the project several times (letting project dry between spraying) before removing the magnets. Mount completed cards on sheets of construction paper; then display on a bulletin board entitled "May The Force Be With You!"

Magnet Man's Exploration Center

In this learning center, Magnet Man encourages students to learn about magnets through hands-on experiences. Cut out each task card (pages 35-38). Fold each card in half, glue together, and laminate. Each task requires magnets, common classroom materials, and a student recording sheet (page 39). Label these supplies (listed to the right) and display them along with the task cards. Then encourage students to visit the center and select from among Magnet Man's seven learning tasks.

Supplies needed:

- **magnet assortment**—must include a horseshoe magnet labeled 1, a bar magnet labeled 2, and a bar magnet labeled 3. Prepare magnet 3 for Task Card 6 by snugly tying a 12-inch length of yarn around the magnet. Additional magnets do not need to be labeled.

- **three large Ziploc® bags**—Label and fill bag 1 with an assortment of magnetic and nonmagnetic items such as a key, an eraser, a brad, a paper clip, a pushpin, a screw, and a metal nut. Label and fill bag 2 with two dozen paper clips. Label and fill bag 3 with ten paper plates and one paper clip.

- **also include**—duplicated copies of the student recording sheet on page 39, a pencil, an iron nail, and a heavy book.

Susan Fink—Gr. 1, Valentine Elementary School, Valentine, NE

Task Card #1

What do magnets look like?

You need:
magnets

Do this:
Look at the magnets.
Draw each magnet on your paper.

Magnets come in all shapes and sizes. Some are horseshoe-shaped. Some are round and some are shaped like rectangles. You may not see them but magnets are serving useful purposes all around you.

Write what you found out.

Task Card #2

What will magnets attract?

You need:
magnet 1 or 2   bag 1

Do this:
Take the items out of the bag.
Use the magnet to try to pick up each item.
If the item is "attracted" draw it on your paper.

Things made of iron, steel, nickel, or cobalt are attracted to a magnet. Things that were picked up by your magnet must have been made of iron, steel, nickel, or cobalt.

Write what you found out.

36

Task Card #3

Are some magnets stronger than others?

You need:
magnet 1   bag 2
magnet 2

Do this:
Hold magnet 1. Put one paper clip on the magnet. Now put a paper clip on the first paper clip. Keep adding paper clips to make a chain. Write the number of paper clips in the chain.

Now do this:
Hold magnet 2. Put paper clips on this magnet to make a chain. Write the number of paper clips in the chain.

Write what you found out.

Some magnets are stronger than others.

Task Card #4

Are magnets stronger near the poles (ends)?

You need:
magnet 2   bag 2

Do this:
Hang a paper clip chain from the middle of the magnet. Write the number of paper clips in the chain.

Now do this:
Hang a paper clip chain from one end of the magnet. Write the number of paper clips in the chain.

Write what you found out.

Magnets are stronger near the poles (ends).

Task Card #5

Can magnets attract through other things?

> Magnets can attract things through other things.

You need:
magnet 2   bag 3

Do this:
Place the paper clip on a paper plate. Hold the magnet under the plate. Move the magnet. Write what happens.

Now do this:
Add a paper plate to the first plate. Move the magnet. If the paper clip moves, add another plate. How many plates can you add and still move the clip using the magnet?

Write what you found out.

Task Card #6

Do the poles (ends) of magnets repel or attract?

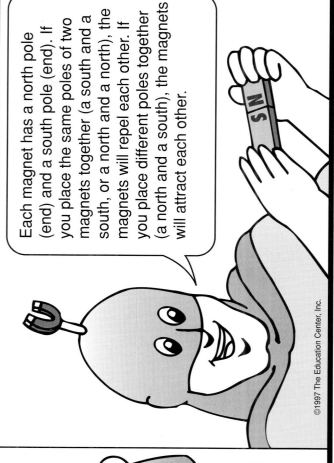

> Each magnet has a north pole (end) and a south pole (end). If you place the same poles of two magnets together (a south and a south, or a north and a north), the magnets will repel each other. If you place different poles together (a north and a south), the magnets will attract each other.

You need:
magnet 2   magnet 3   a heavy book

Do this:
Dangle magnet 3 over the edge of a table. Put one end of magnet 2 by one end of magnet 3. Write what happens.

Now do this:
Hold the other end of magnet 2 by the same end of magnet 3. Write what happens.

Write what you found out.

All things are made of molecules. A magnet's molecules all face one direction. Things made of iron or steel can be made into magnets. As you rubbed the nail on the magnet all the molecules in the nail lined up in the same direction. This made the nail into a magnet, too!

Task Card #7

Can you make a temporary magnet?

You need:
magnet 2   an iron nail   Magnet Man

Do this:
Rub the nail on the magnet at least 50 times. Be sure to rub the nail in the same direction each time.

Now do this:
With the nail, try to pick up Magnet Man. If the temporary magnet won't pick him up, repeat the directions above.

Write what you found out.

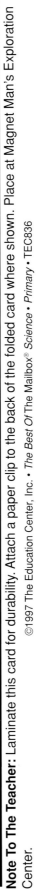

Note To The Teacher: Laminate this card for durability. Attach a paper clip to the back of the folded card where shown. Place at Magnet Man's Exploration Center.

©1997 The Education Center, Inc. • *The Best Of The Mailbox® Science • Primary* • TEC836

Name _____ Task Card #_____

Magnet Man's
Exploration Center

What I am trying to find out:

_____

_____

My work:

What I found out:

_____

_____

_____

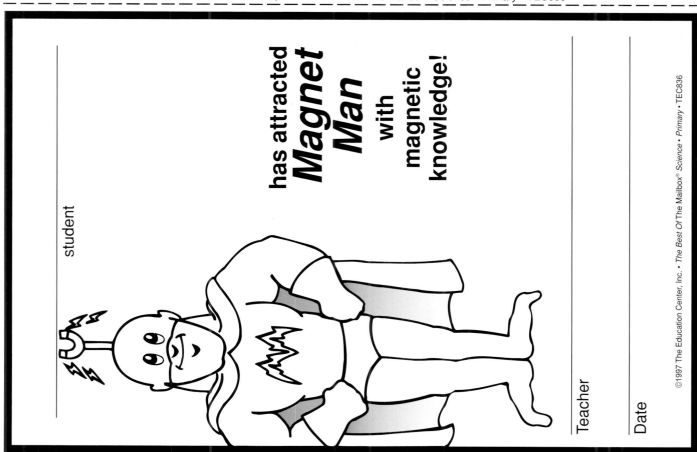

Note To The Teacher: Use the student recording sheet with "Magnet Man's Exploration Center" on page 39. Duplicate and present the Magnet Man awards to students as desired.

A Pocketful Of Science

In The Know About Snow And Ice

Use the following hands-on activities to explore the wonders of snow and ice.

ideas by Ann Flagg

Activity 1: A Chilling Mystery

You will need:
large resealable plastic bag
snow or crushed ice
large brown grocery bag
one plastic cup per student
science experience chart
(See illustration.)

Observation Using The Five Senses	
sight	
touch	
smell	
taste	
hearing	

What to do:

Without your youngsters' knowledge, fill the plastic bag with clean snow or crushed ice; then securely seal the bag and place it inside the brown bag.

First have students observe the brown bag and predict its contents. Next ask a student to grasp the top of the bag with both hands and describe the bag's weight. Enlist several students to reach inside the bag and feel and describe the contents. Display a chart like the one shown and record your youngsters' observations on it. Have students continue observing and predicting. When the correct prediction is made, reveal the contents of the plastic bag. Give each student a small portion of the snow or ice in a plastic cup. Have students continue to observe the frozen matter using their five senses as you record their observations on the chart.

Avoid misconceptions:

In Activities 1, 3, and 4, it is suggested that crushed ice be used if snow is not available. Although snow and ice are both frozen water, they are not the same. The frozen crystals in snow are interspersed with greater amounts of air than the frozen crystals in ice. In other words, ice crystals have less air between them. This is why snow melts more quickly than ice.

Activity 2: Snowflakes Or No Flakes?

You will need:
student copies of page 42   pencils
a supply of tissue-paper squares   scissors

What to do:

Distribute the student activity pages. Explain that all snowflakes have something in common and challenge students to discover this characteristic. To begin, have students find the first crystal on their papers. Explain that this crystal *is* a snowflake. Have students carefully observe the crystal and write "yes" on the line. Explain that the second crystal *is not* a snowflake. Have students carefully observe this crystal and write "no" on the line. Continue examining the illustrated crystals as a group until the common characteristic (all snowflakes have six sides) is identified. Help students understand the importance of guessing in the problem-solving process; then have students complete the remainder of the page independently. Conclude the lesson by having students fold and cut out an assortment of unique tissue-paper snowflakes for decorating the classroom. Be sure that students understand that no two snowflakes are alike!

This is why:

All snow crystals have six sides and are either flat and platelike or long and columnar in shape. It is believed to be impossible for two snowflakes to be identical, because they would have to fall through exactly the same air temperature and moisture levels on their way to earth in order to be the same. This is highly unlikely. However, in 1988 Nancy Wright, a physicist, caught two seemingly identical snowflakes. Examining large photos of the snowflakes revealed no differences. Ms. Wright believes the differences may have been so slight that they could not be detected.

Activity 3: Dig In!

You will need:
The Snowy Day by Ezra Jack Keats (published by The Viking Press)
hot pot
tablespoon
large plastic mixing bowl
snow or crushed ice
access to a freezer
five clear plastic cups

What to do:
Early in the day read aloud The Snowy Day. Ask students what they think happened to Peter's snowball. Fill the bowl with snow (or crushed ice) and ask students to predict what will happen to the snow (ice) if it is left in the classroom. Display the bowl in a prominent location and encourage students to share the changes they observe as the day progresses.

In the afternoon, gather students around the bowl of melted matter. Pour two tablespoons of the liquid into each cup. Place the cups in the freezer. Twenty minutes later, divide students into five groups and give each group a cup. Have the groups closely observe the contents of their cups; then return the cups to the freezer. Repeat this procedure two more times. After each observation session, have students share their observations and discuss the transformation that is taking place.

While the cups of melted snow are transforming into frozen matter, demonstrate another water form. To do this, pour the water that remains in the large bowl into a hot pot and bring it to a boil. Have students observe the rising water vapor.

This is why:

Water can be a solid, a liquid, or a gas. Freezing *is the process of a liquid changing to a solid by the removal of heat. Water freezes at 32° F. The children should begin to notice crystals in the cups after the first 20 minutes. When water is boiled it turns into a vapor called* steam. *Water boils at 212° F.*

Activity 4: Easy Snow Cream

You will need:
two 14-oz. cans of sweetened condensed milk
two quarts of half-and-half
six resealable plastic bags
six 1-lb. coffee cans with plastic lids
six 3-lb. coffee cans with plastic lids
snow or crushed ice
one spoon and one small cup per student
measuring cup
masking tape
salt

What to do:
Mix together the milk and the half-and-half. Pour two cups of the mixture into each resealable bag. Securely seal the bags; then place each bag in a small can. Snap a lid on each can and secure it with masking tape. Place each small can inside a larger can. Pack the open space in each larger can with a mixture of five parts ice to one part salt. Snap a lid on each can and secure it with masking tape.

Divide students into six groups and give each group a can. Have each group sit on the floor and roll its can back and forth for approximately ten minutes. Then help each group carefully check the contents of its smaller can. Encourage students to share and discuss their observations. Next empty each large can and repack the smaller can inside, using a fresh mixture of ice and salt. Secure all lids with masking tape.

Instruct each group to roll its can for ten more minutes. Then remove the smaller cans and observe the snow cream inside. Serve the snow cream using the spoons and cups.

Questions to ask:
1. How did the milk mixture change?
2. Why did this change happen?
3. Why was the salt added to the ice?

This is why:

By lowering the temperature of the milk mixture, it changed from a liquid matter to a solid matter. The milk mixture became frozen at approximately 27° F. The ice alone could only lower the temperature to 32° F. Adding salt lowered the temperature of the ice so that the milk substance could freeze.

Name _____

Spotting Snowflakes

Look carefully at each shape below.
If it **is** a snowflake, write **yes**.
If it **is not** a snowflake, write **no**.

1.	2.	3.
4.	5.	6.
7.	8.	9.
10.	11.	12.

Note To Teacher: Use with "Activity 2: Snowflakes Or No Flakes?" on page 40.

Positively
PENGUINS

For birds that can't fly, penguins sure know how to get around! So why not follow their lead and dive headlong into this collection of penguin-related activities and reproducibles? There's no doubt that you and your youngsters will discover that these fine-feathered fowl are definitely cool!

Vacancy At The South Pole

Contrary to popular belief, penguins do not live at the South Pole. Penguins are seabirds, and the South Pole lies 800 miles from the nearest ocean. That's a long walk to dinner—even for a penguin! Penguins do, however, live in the Southern Hemisphere. Those that prefer the colder climates live on the shores of Antarctica. The Falkland Islands and South Georgia in the Atlantic Ocean (off the southern tip of South America) are home to millions of penguins. And penguins also live on the southern coasts of Africa, Australia, and New Zealand. Some penguins even live on the western coast of South America. And the most tropical of all penguins live on the Galapagos Islands, just south of the equator! For a clear picture of penguin habitats, have students complete the penguin mapping activity on page 46.

Sizing Up Penguins

Penguins come in a variety of sizes. The world's largest penguin, the emperor, stands approximately 45 inches tall and can weigh close to 100 pounds. The smallest penguin is the little blue, or fairy, penguin. It measures in at just over a foot tall and weighs about two pounds. The reproducible student activity on page 47 gives students an opportunity to learn more about penguin sizes as they read and interpret information on a bar graph.

To follow up this activity, write the penguin names from the page on tagboard strips. Divide students into five groups and give each group a different penguin name. Ask each group to measure and display its strip on a designated wall at the actual height of the penguin. Challenge students to locate similar information about other penguin species. You'll soon have a parade of penguin facts!

Cool Swimwear

Penguins—who spend over half of each year in the water—sport perfect swimwear for the chilly conditions they face. Their small, stiff feathers snugly overlap each other, keeping out freezing winds and water. These feathers—about 70 of them per square inch—completely cover a penguin's body. Beneath this layer of scale-like feathers is a second layer of woolly down. Penguins also have a thick layer of blubber under their skin that helps to keep them warm.

For a bit of counting fun and a firsthand look at the small size of penguin feathers, give each student a quarter-page of one-inch graph paper. Challenge each student to draw 70 overlapping feathers in one square on his paper. If his square becomes full before he reaches 70, have him record the number of feathers he drew in an adjacent square. Then have him choose a blank square and repeat the activity. You may find the strategies that your students employ to squeeze 70 feathers into a square inch quite enlightening!

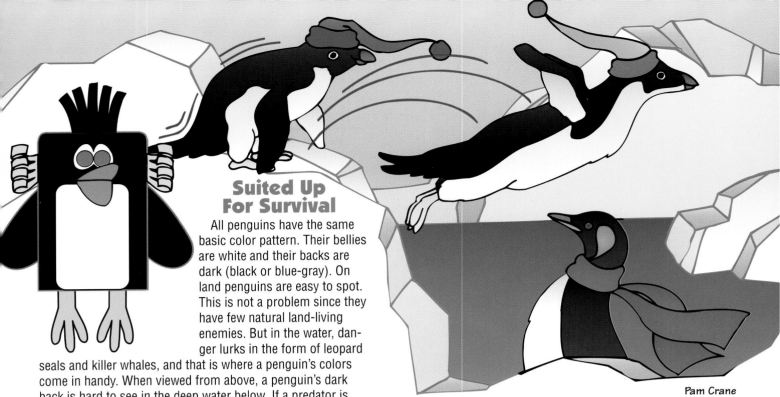

Suited Up For Survival

All penguins have the same basic color pattern. Their bellies are white and their backs are dark (black or blue-gray). On land penguins are easy to spot. This is not a problem since they have few natural land-living enemies. But in the water, danger lurks in the form of leopard seals and killer whales, and that is where a penguin's colors come in handy. When viewed from above, a penguin's dark back is hard to see in the deep water below. If a predator is swimming below a penguin, it may not notice the bird because the penguin's white belly blends into the brightness of the sunlit ocean's surface.

These easy-to-make, construction-paper puppets can be made and used by students to further investigate penguin *camouflage.* To make a puppet, roll a 9" x 12" sheet of black paper into a cylinder and glue it. Position the seam at the back of the project, and glue the top one inch of the cylinder closed. When the top dries, trim to round each of the glued corners. Next trim to round each corner of a 4" x 6" sheet of white paper and carefully glue the resulting penguin belly to the front of the project. Fold in half a 3" x 9" strip of black paper and cut out two matching wings. Glue the wings to the body. Then—from scraps of red, orange, yellow, black, and white paper—cut out and glue on the feet, beak, facial features, and head markings of your favorite penguin species.

Handsome Headbands

There are 18 or so different penguin species (scientists disagree over the exact number), and each penguin species has a unique head marking or *headband.* Scientists believe the head markings help penguins recognize their own species and stay together.

The booklet project on page 48 introduces five different species of penguins and their distinguishable head markings. Duplicate student copies of the page on white construction paper. To make a booklet, a student reads the text on each booklet page (or has it read to him) and colors the penguin picture to match. After completing the booklet cover, he cuts on the dotted lines, and stacks and staples the booklet cover and pages together. Encourage students to design additional pages for their booklets as they learn about different penguin species.

I am a rockhopper penguin. I have red eyes. Yellow feathers poke out from the sides of my head. I have short black feathers on my head. My beak is orange.

Pam Crane

Bird Or Fish?

Long ago, when an explorer saw penguins for the first time, he thought he had discovered feathered fish! Unlike most birds, penguins are excellent swimmers. They spend large amounts of time in the water and return to land only to molt or to have and raise their young. Scientists believe that there is a direct connection between the wonderful swimming abilities of penguins and the fact that they can not fly. For example, penguins need wings that are too small for flying and they need bodies that are too heavy for flying, in order to be excellent swimmers. These hands-on experiments can help students better understand these concepts.

Heavy Bodies For Swimming

To show that the heavy body of a penguin is better suited for swimming and diving than the light body of a flying bird, you will need a plastic dishpan partially filled with water and two empty 35-mm film canisters. Fill one canister with sand; then snap the lids on both of the canisters and place them in the tub of water. Point out that one canister floats lower in the water. Compare the two canisters to the bodies of a penguin and a flying bird. Explain that a penguin has solid bones (the sand-filled canister), which are heavier than the hollow bones (the empty canister) of a flying bird.

Next gently push down on both canisters using equal force. As you do this, explain that the heavier canister is easier to push down into the water. Help students conclude that the extra weight makes it easier to push the canister into the water. In a similar way, it is easier for a penguin to dive than it is for a lighter bird. Place these supplies and plenty of paper towels at a center for individual student exploration.

Small Wings For Swimming

To show the efficiency of small wings over large wings for swimming, you will need a plastic dishpan partially filled with water and two pieces of 8 1/2" x 11" paper. Fold one sheet of paper five or six times. First use the unfolded paper to try to paddle the water back and forth in the pan. Then repeat this step using the folded paper. The folded paper, like a penguin's wing, pushes the water better. Place the dishpan of water, a supply of 8 1/2" x 11" paper, and a trash can at a center for individual student exploration.

Me, me, mooooooo. ④

It's All In The Call

Have you ever wondered how a penguin finds its mate or child in a group of 2,000 look-alikes? It's all in the call. Each penguin has its own voice or call. Just like people, penguins can recognize each other by their voices. When penguin parents return from the sea with food, they call out for their young. In a similar manner, penguin partners reunite at the beginning of the mating season. Penguin voices are loud, so their rookeries are quite rowdy!

If you're willing to endure a bit of noise yourself, your youngsters will enjoy and learn from this simulation activity. Label individual paper slips (one per student) with fictitious penguin calls such as "Me, me, mooooooo," and "Lo, lo, leeeee!" Label the strips in sets of three or four—using the identical call on each strip in a set. (Also note the number of strips in each set as shown.) Then bundle up your youngsters and take them outdoors, or head to the school gymnasium or cafeteria. Randomly distribute the paper slips and on a given signal, have students use their penguin calls to find their penguin families. Once a family is united, it sits together in a predesignated "quiet zone." When all penguins have found their families, return to the classroom. Perhaps a snack of goldfish-shaped crackers and penguin punch (the beverage of your choice) would be in order.

Cooperation Pays Off

Even penguins know that working together brings positive results. During the frigid winter months, penguins work together to stay warm. To do this, the birds stand with their backs to the wind huddled together in a triangle shape. By packing themselves together (as many as ten emperor penguins in one square yard!), they can share their body heat and shield one another from the cold and wind. In addition, the penguins rotate places within the triangle so that the penguins on the perimeter of the triangle also spend time in the center of the triangle where it is warmest.

Students can feel the heat of this cooperation technique indoors or outdoors. In a large open area, arrange students shoulder-to-shoulder in the shape of a large triangle. Position students so that their backs are to an imaginary or real wind source. Slowly have the youngsters on the perimeter of the triangle between points B and C (see the diagram) move to the point (or corner) nearest them, then move forward to point A. Continually repeat this procedure until the students who began the activity on the perimeter of the triangle between points B and C return to that general area. Then have students sit on the floor momentarily to discuss what they have learned. Ask the youngsters questions like "Why were some places within the triangle warmer than others?"; "When penguins are protecting themselves from the cold in this manner, why do they move around rather than just stand still?"; and "What situations can you think of where humans could benefit by grouping together like this?"

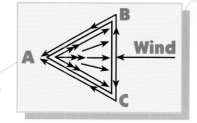

A Family Affair

Regardless of the penguin species, with these birds, raising their young is a family affair. Compare and contrast how different penguin species prepare for, incubate, and raise their young. If desired, compile the information you uncover on a class graph. Stimulate student interest with the following information; then challenge your youngsters to uncover more facts about a variety of penguin species.

- *Magellan* penguins make nests by digging holes with their feet and beaks. Then they line the holes with grass.
- *Gentoos* make bowl-shaped nests from rocks. The female gentoo lays two eggs. The second egg is laid three days after the first egg. Both the male and the female incubate the eggs.
- Instead of building nests, *king* penguins turn their backs to the wind and hold their eggs (one per couple) under their bodies. Soon after an egg is delivered, the male takes over caring for the egg while the female returns to the ocean to feed.
- *Rockhopper* penguins lay two eggs. The first egg is always much smaller and it rarely hatches.

A Few Words About Penguins

Students put their penguin vocabularies to the test with this hands-on project. Each student will need a white construction-paper copy of pages 49 and 50, crayons, scissors, glue, a brad, and a small, dark-colored button. To complete the penguin project, read the word clues on page 50, and cut out and glue the matching words in place. Next cut out the three strips and glue them together as indicated. Set the resulting vocabulary strip aside. Color and cut out the patterns on page 49. Glue the top of the vocabulary strip to the body where indicated; then accordion-fold the rest of the strip. Use the brad to attach the wing to the penguin body at the dot; then position the wing over the folded paper strip to hold the strip in place. Finally glue the button eye in place. Now there's a brilliant bird!

A Few Words About Penguins

Cool Colonies

Penguins live on land near cold water.
Color the map key. Use three different colors.
Use the map key to color the map.

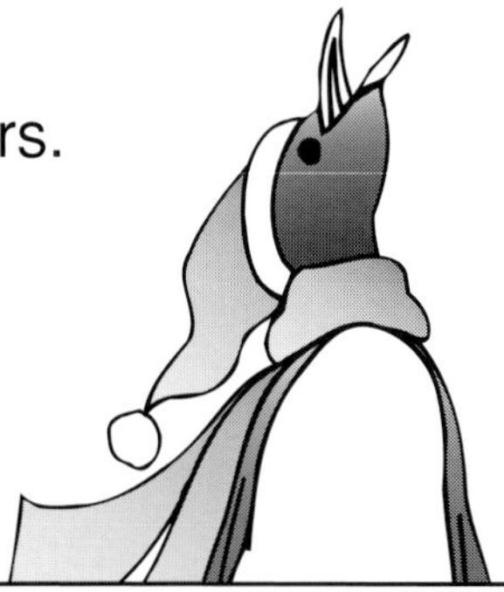

Map Key

☐ equator
☐ where penguins do not live
☐ where penguins live:

Falkland Islands
South Georgia
Antarctica (shorelines)
Africa (southern coast)

Australia (southern coast)
New Zealand (southern coast)
South America (western coast)
Galapagos Islands

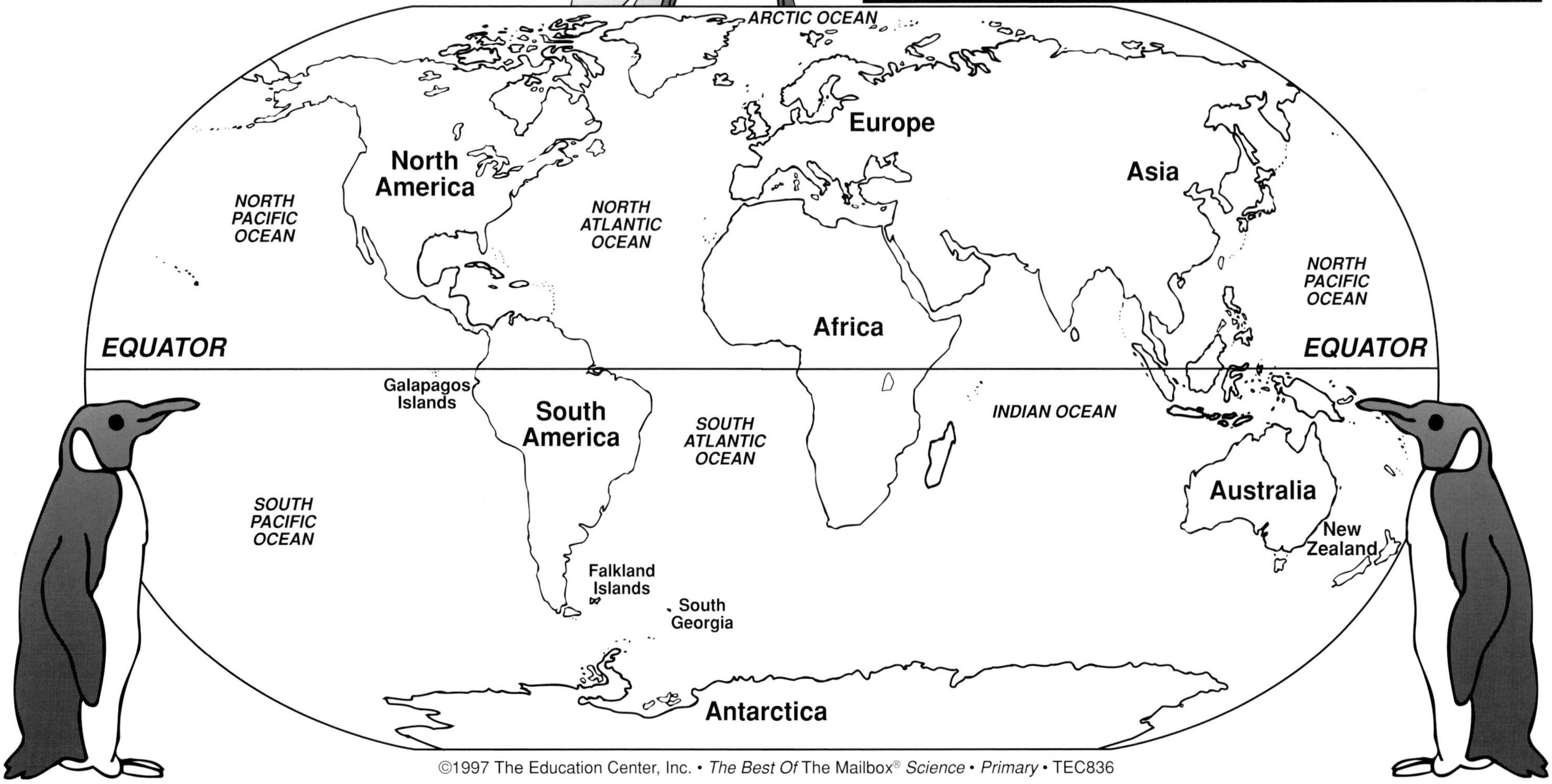

EQUATOR

NORTH PACIFIC OCEAN

Australia

New Zealand

INDIAN OCEAN

Asia

Europe

ARCTIC OCEAN

Africa

SOUTH ATLANTIC OCEAN

South Georgia

Falkland Islands

Antarctica

NORTH ATLANTIC OCEAN

North America

South America

Galapagos Islands

NORTH PACIFIC OCEAN

SOUTH PACIFIC OCEAN

EQUATOR

EQUATOR

Name _____

Sizing Up Penguins

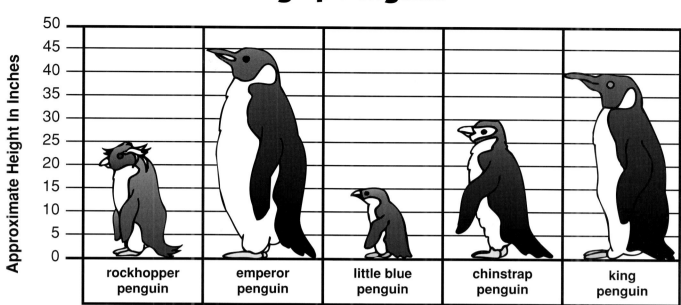

Answer the questions.
Use the graph.

1. Which kind of penguin is 40 inches tall? _____

2. Which two kinds of penguins are taller than the chinstrap penguin?

   _____   _____

3. How tall is the rockhopper penguin? _____

4. Which kind of penguin is about the same size as the rockhopper penguin?

   _____

5. Which kind of penguin is just over one foot tall? _____

6. How many inches taller is the emperor penguin than the little blue penguin?

   _____

7. Which penguin is taller than the rockhopper penguin and shorter than the king penguin? _____

8. Do you think the emperor penguin weighs more than the chinstrap penguin?

   _____ Why? _____

   _____

I am an emperor penguin. My head and eyes are black. I have an orange stripe on my black beak. I have an orange and yellow patch by each ear.

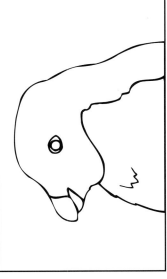

I am a chinstrap penguin. The top of my head is black. My face and throat are white except for a narrow black line that looks like a chinstrap! My beak is black. My eyes are brown.

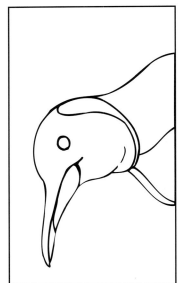

I am a king penguin. I have brown eyes. My beak is black with an orange stripe. My head is black. My neck patches are bright orange.

I am an Adélie penguin. My head is black. So is my beak. I have a white ring around each eye. My eyes are black.

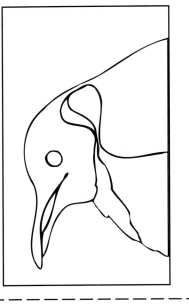

A Parade Of Penguins

Name _____

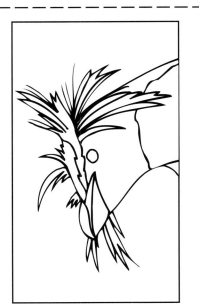

I am a rockhopper penguin. I have red eyes. Yellow feathers poke out from the sides of my head. I have short black feathers on my head. My beak is orange.

Note To Teacher: Use with "Handsome Headbands" on page 44.
©1997 The Education Center, Inc. • *The Best Of The Mailbox® Science • Primary* • TEC836

wing

Use with "A Few Words About Penguins" on page 45.

finished project

A Few Words About Penguins

Glue the top of strip A here.

A

A fast way for penguins to travel on land.

Many penguin chicks squeezing together to stay warm.

Small pink shellfish that are a favorite food of penguins.

Glue strip B here.

B

A place where penguins gather and build their nests.

A pouch of skin where some penguins store their eggs.

When a penguin loses its old feathers as it grows new ones.

Glue strip C here.

C

When penguins "pop" out of the water to breathe while swimming.

The way a penguin walks.

A
Few Words
About
Penguins

porpoising	crèche	
rookery	molting	krill
waddling	brood pouch	tobogganing

©1997 The Education Center, Inc. • *The Best Of* The Mailbox® *Science* • *Primary* • TEC836 • Key p. 159

Note To Teacher: Use with "A Few Words About Penguins" on page 45.

A Pocketful Of Science

Investigating Evergreens

If you're planning to investigate evergreen trees, there's probably no better time than the holiday season. You can easily gather a variety of evergreen sprigs from Christmas tree farms or curbside lots. And since most deciduous trees will have shed their leaves, it's the perfect time to compare and contrast these two types of trees. Doesn't that sound like a "tree-mendous" opportunity that shouldn't be missed?

ideas by Ann Flagg

Activity 1: Introducing Evergreens

You will need:
deciduous and needleleaf evergreen trees or sprigs from each
cones and needles that have been shed from evergreen trees

What to do:
Ask students to feel the needles of the evergreen tree. If you have taken your youngsters outdoors to an actual tree, also have them search the ground around the tree for needles and cones. Or have students examine the needles and cones you have provided. Next have students observe a deciduous tree (or a sprig taken from one). Ask students to compare and contrast these two types of trees.

Questions to ask:
1. Do evergreen trees have leaves? Explain your answer.
2. How do you know that evergreens shed their leaves?
3. Why do most needleleaf evergreen trees have cones?

This is why:

Children may be surprised to learn that the slender needles on the evergreen are its leaves. Needleleaf evergreen leaves look different from the leaves of a deciduous tree, but both leaf-types make food for the tree. An evergreen grows new leaves before it sheds its old ones. This gradual process keeps the tree green throughout the year. Some evergreen trees keep their leaves for several years before shedding them.

Most needleleaf evergreens do not produce flowers; instead they produce cones. The male cones produce pollen. The female cones produce seeds that fall out from between the scales of the cones when they are ripe.

Activity 2: More About Evergreens

You will need:
clippings from broadleaf evergreens
(Broadleaf evergreens include holly, box, myrtle, live oak, rhododendron, laurel, and some magnolia trees and shrubs.)
clippings and cones from needleleaf evergreens
(Needleleaf evergreens include pine, fir, spruce, hemlock, cypress, and yew trees and shrubs.)
display table labeled "Our Evergreen Museum" including:
marker, tape, blank index cards, field guide to trees

What to do:
Display your samples on the table, and explain that all of the clippings were taken from evergreen trees or shrubs. Next have students identify various characteristics of each sample. Then, with your students' assistance, sort the samples into three groups: *needleleaf evergreens, broadleaf evergreens,* and *cones.* Using the marker, write the group names on separate index cards; then tape each card near its group. Encourage students to visit the resulting evergreen museum. Also invite students to add evergreen samples to the collection. To do this, send home a note to parents that briefly states your request and encourages parents to assist their children with this project. Each day have students share any samples they brought from home. Have the students place the samples in the museum and use the materials to label them with the names of the trees and shrubs from which they were taken.

When you have enough evergreen samples, divide students into small groups. Give each group a few broadleaf samples, a few cones, and several needleleaf samples. Ask each group to study its samples and sort them into the three groups: broadleaf evergreens, cones, and needleleaf evergreens.

Questions to ask:
1. Do all evergreens have needles?
2. Did you find any similarities between the broadleaf samples and the needleleaf samples?
3. How are your broadleaf samples alike (different)?
4. How are your needleleaf evergreens alike (different)?
5. Why do you think some evergreen trees have cones?

Next:
Have each group of students sort the samples in its three groups into smaller groups. Accept all reasonable classification systems.

This is why:

There are two types of evergreens: broadleaf evergreens *and* needleleaf evergreens *or* conifers. *Broadleaf trees have broad, flat leaves that are quite unlike the needles and scales of conifers. Both types of evergreens stay green year-round. The leaves of broadleaf trees and the leaves or needles of needleleaf trees vary in size and shape. Some needles grow singly, in pairs, in threes, or in fives. Still others grow in clusters or rosettes. Some needles are scale-like.*

All trees produce seeds. Needleleaf evergreens or conifers produce seeds inside hard cones. These cones protect the seeds until they are fully developed; then the cones fall from the trees. Some cones drop to the ground in one piece. Others fall apart on the tree and fall to the ground in pieces. Broadleaf evergreens protect their seeds inside different types of fruit or nuts. Holly's fruit is bright red berries. Live oak's nut is acorns.

Pam Crane

Follow-up:

Give each student a copy of the booklet on page 53. Have students cut apart and staple the pages in order. To complete his booklet, a student visits the evergreen museum and draws and colors appropriate illustrations on the booklet pages. If desired, make crayons available at the museum.

Activity 3:
Customized For Snow

You will need:
empty, large shaker dispenser (like a Parmesan cheese dispenser)
powdered sugar to partially fill the dispenser
clipping from a needleleaf evergreen
clipping from a broadleaf evergreen
two 12" x 18" sheets of black construction paper

What to do:

Under the watchful eyes of your youngsters, lay the sheets of paper at opposite ends of a tabletop and place one clipping on each. Next enlist a student volunteer to stand at each end of the table. Ask the students to hold the clippings about six inches above the provided papers in positions that are representative of how the clippings were attached to their original plants. (Provide assistance as needed.) With the powdered sugar in the dispenser, make it "snow" by sprinkling the sugar over the clippings. Try to dispense an equal amount of powdered sugar onto each clipping.

Questions to ask:
1. Which paper has the most powdered sugar on it? Why?
2. Which leaf design is better suited for areas that receive heavy snowfall?
3. Do you think you would be more likely to find needleleaf evergreens or broadleaf evergreens growing in snowy areas? Why?

This is why:

The special design of needleleaf evergreens enables them to survive in regions with heavy snowfall. Sloping branches and sturdy needles that are often smooth and flexible shed snow more easily than broad, flat leaves. Because the needles have less surface area than the broad, flat leaves, heavy buildups of snow are less likely—as are broken tree limbs caused by the weight of accumulated snow. Many evergreen needles also have a built-in antifreeze that helps protect them from frost damage.

Activity 4:
Customized For Dryness

For each student, you will need:
three-inch square of waxed paper
three-inch square of paper towel
one or more evergreen needles

For each small group, you will need:
eyedropper
plastic container of blue-tinted water

What to do:

Divide students into small groups and disburse supplies. To begin, ask students to carefully feel their evergreen needles, cautioning them that the ends of the needles may be sharp. Guide students to discover the waxlike coating on the needles and explain that this protective covering is important to the life of needleleaf evergreens. Remind students that water is stored inside a tree's leaves (or needles). To show how a waxlike coating can protect a tree's water supply, have each child place a drop of blue-tinted water on each of his paper squares. Invite students to share and explain the results of their testing experiences.

Questions to ask:
1. Which paper square is more like an evergreen needle? Why?
2. Why do you think the water stored inside an evergreen needle has good protection from hot, dry, and/or windy weather conditions?
3. Do you think all leaves have waxlike coatings? Why or why not?

This is why:

The leaves of a tree are like tiny power stations. But instead of burning fuel, they make fuel. They take in energy in the form of sunlight and use it to turn carbon dioxide and water into sugars. These sugars are then used as fuel for the tree. The waxlike coating on the needles prevents the water that is stored inside from quickly evaporating during hot, dry, and/or windy weather conditions, and this ensures that the tree can continue to make fuel for its survival. This waxlike coating is not found on all leaves; however, you will find it on some broadleaf evergreens such as holly trees and live oak trees.

Name_____

My Little Book About Evergreens

Some evergreens have flat leaves like these.

They are called **broadleaf evergreens.**

1

Some evergreens have needles like these for leaves.

They are called **needleleaf evergreens.**

2

Evergreen needles have many different shapes.

Some look like this.

3

Others look like this,

and this!

4

Most needleleaf evergreens have **cones.** The cones are different shapes and sizes. Some look like these.

5

Note To Teacher: Use this activity after completing "Activity 2: More About Evergreens" on page 51.

Exploring The Arctic Tundra

Arctic tundra—the very phrase echoes with the thundering emptiness of endless stretches of vast, frozen wasteland. But take another look! The earth's tundra is not as desolate as it first appears. In fact, it's a fragile ecosystem that supports an intricate web of life. Use this collection of activities to visit a biome that beckons to be explored.

ideas contributed by Laura Horowitz

Where Is It?

The tundra is a rolling plain that spreads across the northernmost edge of each continent surrounding the Arctic Ocean. It begins wherever the great forests of the North end. From there it continues to the Arctic Coast and the islands offshore. The tundra covers much of the coast of Alaska, and in Canada it reaches south of the Arctic Circle deep into North America. Use the mapping activity on page 57 to introduce your youngsters to the tundra. When this activity has been completed, turn the maps into journal covers by following the directions in "A Treeless Wonder?"

A Treeless Wonder?

The word *tundra* means "treeless," and that pretty much describes this chilly northern location. The few trees that do grow on the tundra are either growing in sheltered valleys or are not recognizable. Why? Because a 100-year-old tree on the tundra can be less than one foot tall! Your study of the tundra is sure to reveal many more amazing facts. Have students record this tundra fact and others in journals entitled "Amazing, But True! Facts About The Tundra." To make these "tundra-rific" journals, have each child cut out his completed map project from page 57 and mount it on a 9" x 12" sheet of construction paper. After each child has titled and personalized his journal cover, have him staple several sheets of blank paper between his cover and a second sheet of 9" x 12" construction paper. Ready, set, write!

Tundra Talk

Set the stage for lots of Arctic antics by inviting your students to choose tundra-related names for team and small-group activities. Suggest names like *Cool Caribou, Eager Ermines, Wise Wolves,* and *Magnificent Musk Oxen;* then invite students to brainstorm additional names. The thematic names could also be assigned to rows or clusters of student desks: "The Happy Hares may now line up!"

The Changing Seasons

The seasons of the year on the tundra are probably very different from the seasons your youngsters normally experience. Travel to the tundra, and briefly step into each of its seasons with this activity. Give each student four 3 1/2" x 9" strips of white construction paper, and ask him to write the name of a different season at the top of each one. As a class talk about each tundra season. (If desired, begin your discussion by sharing the seasonal information below.) Conclude each discussion by asking the students to illustrate the season on their appropriately labeled strip. To complete this project, have each youngster mount his four illustrations in seasonal order on a 12" x 18" sheet of black construction paper. Display the eye-catching projects on a bulletin board entitled "A Year On The Tundra."

Fall: Autumn on the tundra is very brief. Animals are busy feasting on the remaining seeds and berries. By the end of September, there is snow on the ground. The ground squirrel begins to dig its winter den, and the caribou gather in herds to start their trip back into the forest. The air turns colder and colder. Winter is almost here.

Winter: The tundra looks deserted, but wait! Even in the bitter cold, the white-coated Arctic foxes and wolves must search for food. A snowy owl is preparing to swoop down on a little, white-furred lemming. The nights gradually get longer until— for more than a week—the sun doesn't even shine! Brrr! It's 50° below zero!

Spring: March, April, and May—it should be *spring!* But on the tundra there is still snow on the ground. The days are getting longer. The animals can feel the snow softening. Soon there will be lots of melted snow. Geese begin to arrive. So do ducks, swans, and millions of other birds. They are coming to the tundra to build their nests. Caribou also begin their trek to the tundra.

Summer: At last the snow is gone and the tundra is coming alive! Plants are pushing up out of the soil; flowers are beginning to bloom. Insects that were frozen are now searching for food. Many Arctic animals are losing their winter coats and growing lighter coats for the summer. Caribou, foxes, wolves, bears, and ermines are having babies. Look! There's a butterfly! The days are long, sunny, and cool.

A Tundra Tune

Adapt these Arctic lyrics to the tune of "My Bonnie Lies Over The Ocean." For even more frosty fun, invite your tundra explorers to compose additional verses.

There are bears and hares on the tundra,
Musk oxen and Arctic wolves, too.
They roam on the plains of the tundra,
With deer that are called caribou.

Chorus:
Arctic tundra—a cold place without many trees!
Arctic tundra—a cold place without many trees!

A fox hunts its food on the tundra.
A lemming escapes underground!
Some creatures that live on the tundra,
Are often not there all year round.

Chorus

The winter is cold on the tundra.
There's darkness all the day through.
When summer comes to the tundra,
The sun shines all day—it's true!

Chorus

It never gets warm on the tundra.
The temperature's cold all year.
If you plan to visit the tundra,
Dress warmly and cover your ears!

Animals Of The Arctic

When students complete this booklet project, Arctic animals will be popping up everywhere! To make each booklet page:

1. Color and cut out a picture of an Arctic animal (patterns on pages 59 and 60). Set the cutout aside.
2. Fold in half a 9" x 12" sheet of construction paper.
3. Center a 1 1/2" x 2 1/2" tagboard rectangle on the fold and draw two 2 1/2" lines.
4. Remove the rectangle and cut on the resulting lines.
5. Unfold the paper to a 90° angle. Pull the narrow strip forward and crease it in the opposite direction from the fold.
6. Glue the cutout from step 1 to the front of the protruding strip; then write a fact or two about the animal below the picture.

To compile the pages into a booklet, stack the pages so that the folds are aligned. Starting with the top two pages, glue the pages back-to-back, making sure that the folds stay in line. To make a cover, fold in half a 10" x 14" piece of construction paper. Slip the glued booklet pages inside the folded cover, and glue them in place. Decorate the booklet cover as desired.

musk ox

The musk ox's fur has two layers. The inner, woolly fur keeps in body heat, and the long, outer hairs keep out wind and water.

Arctic Plants

Here's a fun way to explore plant life of the tundra. Duplicate page 58 for your students and yourself. As your youngsters prepare their lotto gameboards, cut apart the plants on your copy of the page and place the cutouts in a container. Give each youngster 20 miniature marshmallows or yogurt-covered raisins to use as game markers. To play, announce the type of game to be played such as "Three in a row," "Four corners," or "Five in a row." Then, one at a time, draw a cutout from the container and name the featured plant. Each student places a marker on the corresponding square on her gameboard. If desired, have the winner of the first game become the caller of the second game and so on. At the conclusion of the activity—while students are munching on their game markers—talk about plant life on the tundra. Discuss how the tundra's short growing season affects plant life; then challenge your tundra explorers to dig up other interesting information about Arctic plants!

A Very Cool Life

Take a class vote to find out how many students think they would enjoy living on the tundra. Invite youngsters to share what they think would be the advantages and disadvantages of such a life. Students may be surprised to discover that many groups of people live on the Arctic tundra. Some of these people have always lived in the Arctic and are called *natives*. Many others have moved to the Arctic.

An Arctic Community by Bobbie Kalman and William Belsey (Crabtree Publishing Company, 1993) is an excellent reference for learning about the current lifestyle of Arctic dwellers. This resource is packed with interesting information and appealing photographs. Students will enjoy finding the similarities and differences between their own lifestyles and those of youngsters their age who live in the Arctic.

Postcards From The Tundra

Culminate your study of the tundra with this postcard-writing activity. Cut a supply of postcards from tagboard. Each card must be of legal mailing size—from 3.5" x 5" to 4.25" x 6". Have each youngster illustrate the front of his tagboard postcard with a tundra scene or a favorite tundra animal. Then—on the back of his card—in the upper left-hand corner, ask him to write a brief, informative caption about his illustration. Next have each youngster write a message to a family member or a friend in which he tells about his "visit" to the tundra. Help the students address their cards; then collect the cards, affix the proper postage, and place the cards in the mail. The recipients of these cards are sure to feel extra special indeed!

Name _____

Touring The Tundra

Use the code to color the map.

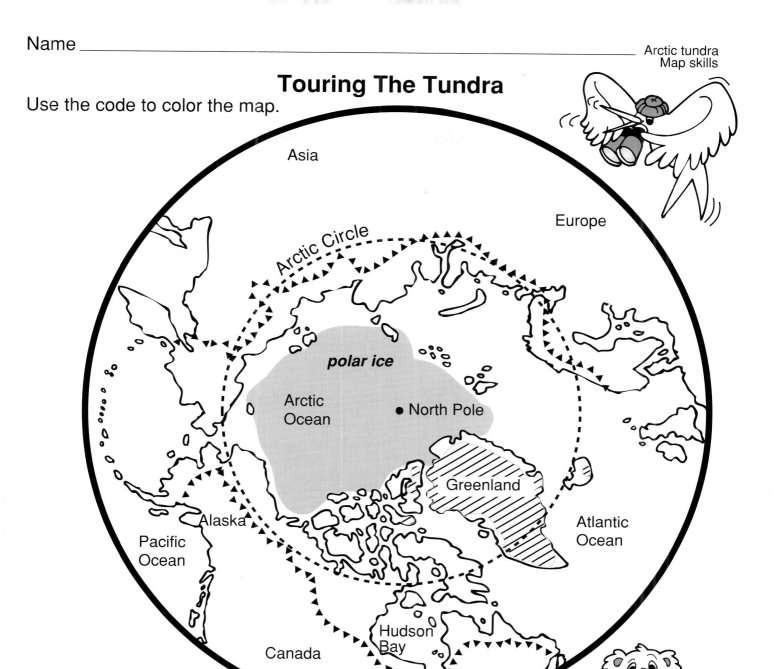

tree line= ▲ ▲ ▲

ice cap= ▨

Color Code

tree line = green   tundra = brown
Arctic Circle = purple North Pole = red
land that is not tundra = yellow water = blue

Note To Teacher: Use with "Where Is It?" and "A Treeless Wonder?" on page 54.

Name _____

Summertime Plants

Make a lotto gameboard.
Color and cut out the plants.
Mix up the plants; then glue each one on the gameboard.

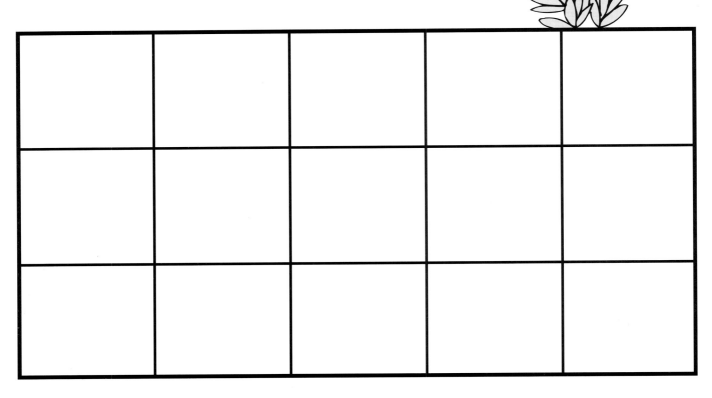

©1997 The Education Center, Inc. • *The Best Of* The Mailbox® *Science* • *Primary* • TEC836

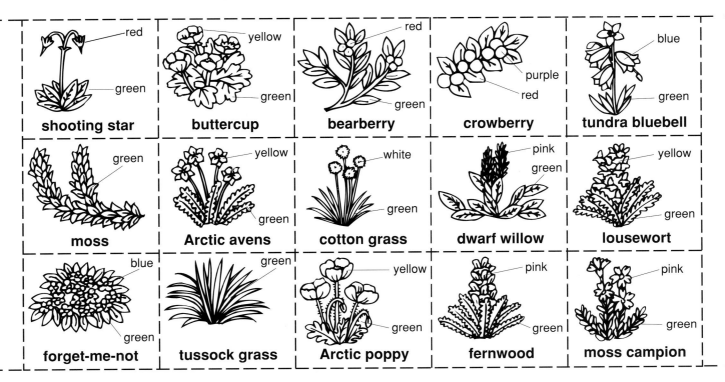

shooting star — red, green
buttercup — yellow, green
bearberry — red, green
crowberry — purple, red
tundra bluebell — blue, green
moss — green
Arctic avens — yellow, green
cotton grass — white, green
dwarf willow — pink, green
lousewort — yellow, green
forget-me-not — blue, green
tussock grass — green
Arctic poppy — yellow, green
fernwood — pink, green
moss campion — pink, green

Note To Teacher: Use with "Arctic Plants" on page 56.

Use with "Animals Of The Arctic" on page 55. For more Arctic animal patterns, see page 60.

caribou

Arctic wolf

musk ox

polar bear

lemming

ptarmigan

Animals are not drawn to scale.

Patterns

Use with "Animals Of The Arctic" on page 55.

snowy owl

Arctic fox

Arctic hare

ermines

seal

Animals are not drawn to scale.

Arctic tern

Robbie Robot's Simple Machines

Put students' thinking skills in high gear with Robbie Robot's collection of hands-on activities! Robbie introduces students to the six simple machines—the lever, inclined plane, screw, wedge, wheel and axle, and pulley—as he challenges students to discover how and why they work.

ideas contributed by Bill O'Connor

Activity 1:
Simple Machines To The Rescue
Reducing Friction

You will need:
four, round pencils   a textbook   a tabletop

What to do:
Place a textbook on a table. Move the textbook back and forth across the table a few times. Then lay the pencils, parallel to one another, on the table. Place the textbook atop the pencils; then move it back and forth a few times.

Questions to ask:
- Was it easier to move the book atop the table or atop the pencils?
- Why do you think the pencils make the book easier to move?
- What do we call something that makes work easier?

Robbie's Reasons:
It was easier to move the book atop the pencils because *friction* was reduced. Friction is the rubbing of one object or surface against another. Machines make work easier because they reduce the amount of friction that occurs.

Activity 2:
Robbie's Ruler Trick
The Lever

You will need:
a wooden ruler   a textbook   a tabletop

What to do:
Lay a ruler on a tabletop so that one end extends over the edge. Lay a textbook atop the opposite end of the ruler. Attempt to lift the book by pressing down on the extended part of the ruler. Repeat this procedure several times. Each time, move the book closer to the table's edge (by pulling on the extended part of the ruler) before pressing down. Continue until the book is at the edge of the table.

Questions to ask:
- How was the book lifted? What kind of simple machine was used?
- Was it easier to lift the book with a long or a short lever? Why?
- What are some other levers?

Robbie's Reasons:
A *lever* was used to lift the book. A lever is a simple machine. It has a strong, stiff bar which rests on a turning point *(fulcrum)*. In this experiment, the ruler acts as a lever and the edge of the table acts as a fulcrum. A lever makes it easier to lift a load. The book was easier to lift with a long lever because the fulcrum was closer to the load. Crowbars, bottle openers, and seesaws are also levers.

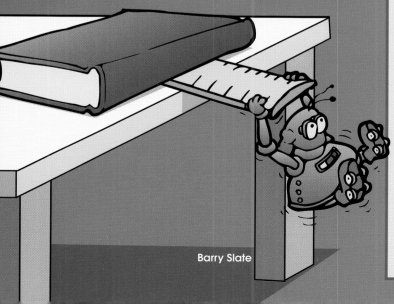

Barry Slate

61

Activity 4:
Robbie's Roll-up
The Screw

You will need:
a right triangle (cut from a nine-inch paper square)
a pencil   a marker
tape   a tabletop

What to do:
Use a marker to outline the diagonal side of the triangle. Hold the triangle perpendicular to the tabletop.

Stop and ask:
• Which simple machine does the triangle look like? *(an inclined plane)*

Then:
Place the triangle facedown on a tabletop. Place the pencil atop one leg of the triangle; then roll the paper around the pencil. Tape the loose end in place.

Questions to ask:
• What simple machine has been made?
• What are some examples of this simple machine?

Robbie's Reasons:
A *screw* was made by winding an inclined plane around in a spiral. The base of a light bulb, a spiral staircase, and a corkscrew are screws.

Activity 3:
Robbie's Race Car Rally
The Inclined Plane

You will need:
five textbooks stacked on a tabletop   two paper clips
a medium-sized toy race car   a yardstick
a medium-sized rubber band

What to do:
Suspend a rubber band from a paper clip; then slide the clip onto one end of a yardstick. Attach the other clip to the race car; then suspend it from the rubber band. Hold the yardstick perpendicular to the tabletop; then lift the yardstick straight up to the top of the stack of books. Record the length of the rubber band. Next reposition the yardstick so it makes a ramp from the tabletop to the top of the book stack. Record the length of the rubber band.

Questions to ask:
• Why was the rubber band more stretched when the perpendicular yardstick was on top of the book stack?
• Which simple machine reduced the stretch of the rubber band?
• What are some other inclined planes?

Robbie's Reasons:
It took more force to lift the car straight up, so the rubber band stretched farther. An ***inclined plane*** decreases the amount of force needed to move something. Because it takes less force to move the race car along an inclined plane, the rubber band is less stretched. Skateboard ramps and slides are inclined planes.

Activity 5:
Robbie's Rap-Tap-Tap
The Wedge

You will need:
a nail   a bolt   a hammer
a block of wood

What to do:
Attempt to hammer the bolt into the block of wood.

Stop and ask:
• Why do you think the bolt can't be hammered into the block of wood?

Then:
Compare the bolt and the nail. Hammer the nail into the block of wood.

Questions to ask:
• Why do you think the nail was easier to hammer into the block of wood?
• Which simple machine made this possible?
• What are some other wedges?

Robbie's Reasons:
The nail was easier to hammer into the wood because it is a *wedge*. A wedge is two inclined planes joined together to form a sharp edge. Most wedges are used to force things apart. Knives, axes, forks, and needles are types of wedges.

Activity 7:
Robbie's Rope Trick
The Pulley

You will need:

two brooms   a length of soft rope

What to do:

Have one student hold a broom parallel to the floor. Have another student hold a broom about 18 inches away from and parallel to the first broom. Tie one end of the rope length to the first broom handle; then loop the rope around both brooms three times. Have a third student slowly pull the loose end of the rope, while the other two students attempt to keep the brooms apart.

Questions to ask:

* Why was it hard to keep the brooms apart?
* What type of simple machine works in a similar way?
* What machines have pulleys?

Robbie's Reasons:

The brooms were hard to keep apart because pulling the rope exerted force on them. Broom handles with a rope looped around them work like a ***pulley***. Pulleys decrease the amount of work needed to lift something. Fishing reels, curtain rods, elevators, and flagpoles have pulleys.

Activity 6:
Round And Round With Robbie
The Wheel And Axle

You will need:

a funnel   a marker   chalk
a ruler

What to do:

Hold the small end of the funnel. Have a student hold the large end. Have the student turn the large end while you try to hold the small end still.

Stop and ask:

* Could the small end be kept still? *(No.)* Why?*(Turning the large end created a very strong force.)*

Then:

Use a marker to make a dot on the large end of the funnel and another one on the small end. Draw an *X* on the floor with chalk. Place the dot on the large end of the funnel atop the *X*. Roll the large end of the funnel one time. Draw an *O* with chalk where it stops. Measure the distance between the *X* and the *O*. Repeat the procedure using the small end of the funnel.

Questions to ask:

* Which end of the funnel traveled the farther distance with one turn?
* Which kind of simple machine makes things easier to turn?
* What are some examples of wheels and axles?

Robbie's Reasons:

The larger end traveled the farther distance. A wheel that turns on a rod is called a ***wheel and axle.*** Less force is needed to turn the wheel and more distance is covered. Turning the axle takes more force and less distance is covered. Doorknobs and pencil sharpeners contain wheels and axles.

Activity 8:
Robbie Reveals A Secret
Compound Machines

You will need:

a pair of scissors   a punch-type can opener   a hand drill
sheets of paper   clean, empty soup cans   two large blocks
                                                          of wood

What to do:

Have students examine and use the scissors and paper, the can opener and soup cans, and the hand drill and wood.

Questions to ask:

* Which simple machines are found in scissors?
* Which simple machines are found in a can opener?
* Which simple machines are found in a hand drill?
* What do you call a machine made up of two or more simple machines?
* What are some other examples of compound machines?

Robbie's Reasons:

Scissors contain two levers (the halves of the scissors) and two wedges (the sharp sides of the blades). A can opener contains a lever (the handle) and a wedge (the punch). A hand drill contains a wheel and axle (the handle), a screw (the bit), and two wedges (the tip and the sharp, spiral edges of the bit). A machine made up of two or more simple machines is called a ***compound machine.*** Bicycles and wheelbarrows are other compound machines.

63

An Out-Of-This-World Adventure!

Exploring The Solar System

If you're planning a study of the solar system, be sure to consider these supplemental literature-based activities before preparing your youngsters for blastoff.

ideas contributed by Wendy Waterman

Postcards From Outer Space

Take a unique trip through the solar system with the help of a one-of-a-kind book entitled *Postcards From The Planets.* This story unfolds as Jessie and Kate depart into space in the year 2095. The twosome chronicle their experiences by writing and sending postcards to their relatives living on Earth. While the book's story line is fictional, the information about the planets has been thoroughly researched. (Available as a Big Book or in packets of six small books each, *Postcards From The Planets* may be purchased from RIGBY publishers by calling 1-800-822-8661.)

After each postcard has been read and discussed, ask your students to choose the solar system locations they would most like to visit. Pair the youngsters according to their preferences; then challenge each twosome to research its destination. To complete the project, have each pair create and complete a postcard like the ones featured in the book. Display the completed projects on a bulletin board entitled "Postcards From Outer Space!"

More About The Solar System

The Planets In Our Solar System by Franklyn M. Branley (published by Thomas Y. Crowell Junior Books) introduces the solar system and its nine planets. The author's simple text enables young readers and listeners to grasp basic facts about the solar system's celestial bodies. In addition directions for making two models of the solar system are given. One model shows the differences in the sizes of the planets. The second model can be displayed on a wall and shows the nine planets and their distances from the sun. Another highly informative book about the solar system is *A Book About Planets And Stars* by Betty Polisar Reigot (published by Scholastic Inc.). Packed with information, this is another book worth considering for your solar system library.

64

Solar System Extravaganza

Showcase an eye-catching reproduction of the solar system on your playground using string, nine tubes (from paper products), and tagboard cutouts to represent the sun and each of the nine planets. Label a tube for each planet. Cut string lengths using the chart below and wrap each length of string around the appropriate tube. Use a hole puncher to punch a hole in the left side of each planet cutout. Punch either one large hole or nine small holes in the right side of the sun cutout. Assign each of nine student groups a planet; then distribute the tubes and planet cutouts to the appropriate groups. On the playground, position the sun cutout in an open area. Seat the students (in their groups) near the sun cutout. Then, in turn, have each group attach one end of its string to the sun cutout and walk away from the sun, gently rolling out the string on its tube. When the string's end is reached, the corresponding planet is attached. Continue in this fashion until all of the planets are displayed. Wow! What a solar system!

Planet	Distance From The Sun	String Length
Mercury	36 million miles	1 yard
Venus	67 million miles	approx. 2 yards
Earth	93 million miles	approx. 2.5 yards
Mars	142 million miles	approx. 4 yards
Jupiter	484 million miles	approx. 13.5 yards
Saturn	885 million miles	approx. 24.5 yards
Uranus	1,780 million miles	approx. 49.5 yards
Neptune	2,790 million miles	approx. 77.5 yards
Pluto	3,660 million miles	approx. 101.5 yards

Jackson Crane

I wish recess was four hours long.

Shooting Stars

The topic of shooting stars—those streaks of light that have long fascinated sky watchers—is sure to evoke an enthusiastic response from your youngsters. Ask students to share their knowledge and questions about shooting stars. Next challenge students to listen carefully as you read aloud *Shooting Stars* by Franklyn M. Branley (published by Thomas Y. Crowell Junior Books). Delightfully illustrated, this informative book explains what shooting stars are, what they are made of, and what happens when they land on Earth. At the conclusion of the book, the author states that some people believe that a wish made upon a shooting star is a wish that will come true.

After reviewing the contents of the book, create this unique class booklet of shooting-star wishes. To make a booklet page, fold a sheet of 9" x 12" construction paper in half and glue the outer edges to form a pocket. Draw and color a night sky scene on the front of the pocket and personalize the back of the pocket. Then, on a slip of paper, write and personalize your wish for a shooting star. Fold the programmed slip in half and tuck it inside the pocket. Bind the pockets between a construction-paper cover labeled "Shooting-Star Wishes." Place the completed project in your classroom library for all to enjoy.

What Is A Black Hole In Space?

Why does lightning continuously flash on Jupiter? Why is Venus's atmosphere so hard to see through? Why do stars twinkle? All of these questions and many more can be answered using the hands-on experiments in Janice VanCleave's *Astronomy For Every Kid: 101 Easy Experiments That Really Work* (published by John Wiley & Sons, Inc.). Written especially for young children, each experiment is presented with its purpose, a list of needed materials, step-by-step instructions, expected results, and a scientific explanation in terms that kids can understand. In fact, each experiment has been "child tested" by the author's own students. Using the experiments in this valuable resource, you can propel your students' science enthusiasm to extraordinary heights!

Out-Of-This-World Poetry

Send your youngsters into orbit with this poetry-writing activity. For an inspiring introduction to space-related poetry, read aloud selected poems from *Space Songs* by poet Myra Cohn Livingston (published by Holiday House, Inc.). Display a length of colorful bulletin-board paper. Write the name of a planet at the top of the paper, and enlist from your youngsters words and phrases that describe the planet. Write each description on the paper, arranging the words in a desired fashion. When the poem is complete, ask students to join in as you read it aloud. Next divide students into small groups and give each group a length of colorful bulletin-board paper and a marker. Working as a team, have each group agree upon a space-related topic and create a poem about it. After each group has shared its poem, post the completed projects in a school hallway for others to enjoy.

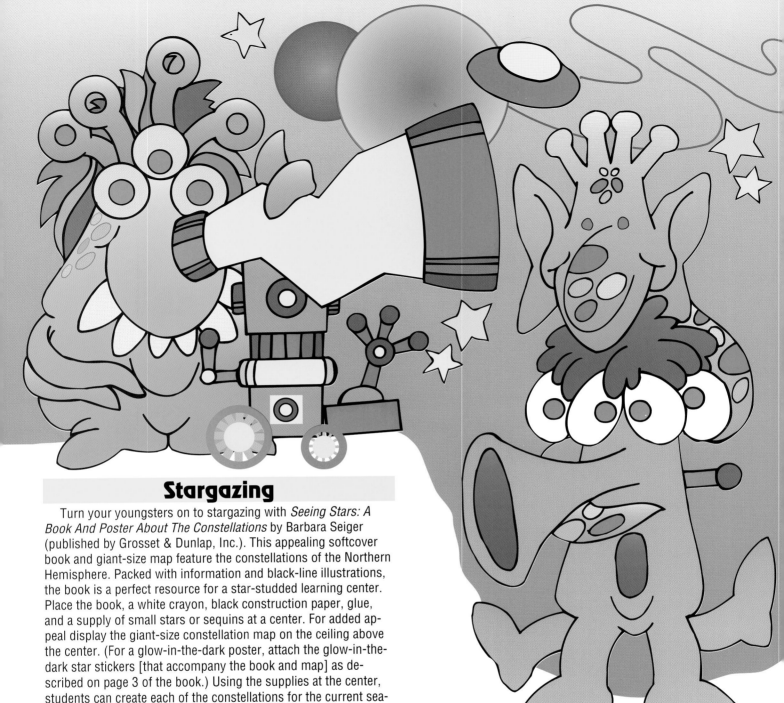

Pam Crane

Stargazing

Turn your youngsters on to stargazing with *Seeing Stars: A Book And Poster About The Constellations* by Barbara Seiger (published by Grosset & Dunlap, Inc.). This appealing softcover book and giant-size map feature the constellations of the Northern Hemisphere. Packed with information and black-line illustrations, the book is a perfect resource for a star-studded learning center. Place the book, a white crayon, black construction paper, glue, and a supply of small stars or sequins at a center. For added appeal display the giant-size constellation map on the ceiling above the center. (For a glow-in-the-dark poster, attach the glow-in-the-dark star stickers [that accompany the book and map] as described on page 3 of the book.) Using the supplies at the center, students can create each of the constellations for the current season. Bind each student's pages between a construction-paper cover, and the student has a personal stargazing guide.

Life On Other Planets

Most youngsters (and adults!) are intrigued by the thought of extraterrestrial neighbors. In Franklyn M. Branley's book *Is There Life In Outer Space?* (published by Thomas Y. Crowell Junior Books), the author discusses several ideas and misconceptions about life in outer space. After reading the book aloud, ask youngsters to recap why most scientists do not believe there is life on the other planets in our solar system. Take a class poll to determine how many students believe that there could be other planets beyond our solar system. Also find out if they think other forms of life may or may not be living on these planets. (See "Alien Artwork" for a far-out follow-up activity!)

Alien Artwork

Send your youngsters into orbit with this totally cosmic project! To set the mood, read aloud a book that features an alien character such as *UFO Diary* by Satoshi Kitamura (published by Farrar Straus Giroux), *Earthlets As Explained By Professor Xargle* by Jeanne Willis (published by E. P. Dutton), or *Space Case* by Edward Marshall (published by Dial Books For Young Readers). Invite each student to imagine the perfect alien and illustrate it on a large sheet of drawing paper. Then have each youngster answer questions about his alien friend by completing a copy of page 67. Be sure to provide time for students to introduce their alien friends to their classmates. Far-out!

Name ______________________ Creative thinking/writing

Introducing An Alien

Answer each question about the alien you illustrated.
Use complete sentences.

1. What is this alien's name? ______________________

2. Where is this alien from? ______________________

3. How old is this alien? ______________________

4. What was this alien's life like before it came to Earth? ______________________

5. What does this alien like to eat? ______________________

6. What does this alien like to do for fun? ______________________

7. What is one thing you hope to learn from your alien friend? ______________________

8. What is one thing you hope to teach your alien friend? ______________________

Note To Teacher: Use this activity with "Alien Artwork" on page 66.

Six Stations From Space

Propel your youngsters' science process skills to extraordinary heights using these hands-on activities. 10..., 9..., 8..., 7..., 6..., 5..., 4..., 3..., 2..., 1..., **Blast off!**

ideas by Ann Flagg

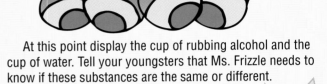

Step One: Preparation

Before introducing this series of science activities to your youngsters, identify and label six numerical workstations in your classroom. Place a magnifying glass, two craft sticks, and several paper towels at each station. You will also need two clear plastic cups per station. Shortly before you introduce the activity, partially fill the plastic cups with the substances listed below. (This must be completed without your youngsters' knowledge.) Then place the partially filled cups at the appropriate workstations.

Station One:	cooking oil and yellow liquid detergent
Station Two:	shaving cream and whipped topping
Station Three:	flour and flour
Station Four:	sugar and salt
Station Five:	flavored drink mix and flavored drink mix
Station Six:	baking powder and baking soda

Step Two: Introduction

You will need:

The Magic School Bus Lost In The Solar System written by Joanna Cole (published by Scholastic Inc.)
one clear plastic cup partially filled with rubbing alcohol
one clear plastic cup partially filled with water
one magnifying glass
two craft sticks
paper towels (for drying fingertips)

What to do:

Read aloud *The Magic School Bus Lost In The Solar System.* Then for a fun lead-in to this collection of hands-on science activities, share the following story-related scenario:

While traveling in the solar system, Ms. Frizzle and her students collected several samples of unknown substances. However when their bus reentered the earth's atmosphere the samples were jostled and mixed up. Ms. Frizzle has asked if our class would help to straighten out this mess.

At this point display the cup of rubbing alcohol and the cup of water. Tell your youngsters that Ms. Frizzle needs to know if these substances are the same or different.

Questions to ask:
1. Who thinks that both cups contain the same (different) substances?
2. Why do you think the substances are the same (different)?

Next:

Based on sight alone, many students may initially think that the liquids are the same. Challenge students to brainstorm other ways the substances could be observed. As additional techniques are suggested and demonstrated by student volunteers, reinforce the following safe science rules:

- Always handle a magnifying glass with extreme care.
- Never taste an unknown substance.
- Never directly inhale an unknown substance. (To smell safely, cup one hand and scoop a handful of vapors from directly above the substance. Bring this handful of air beneath your nose and inhale.)
- Only touch unknown substances with an adult's approval. (Encourage students to touch these substances; however to avoid messy spills do not allow students to place their hands inside the cups. Instead show students how to use a craft stick to remove and place a drop of the substance on a fingertip.)

In conclusion, help students concur as a group that the two substances are different.

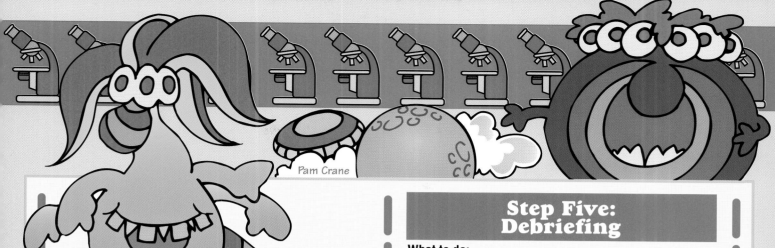

Pam Crane

Step Three:
Final Preparations

You will need:
six pencils
six copies of the observation sheet on page 70

What to do:
Direct your students' attention to the six workstations. Explain that each student will be a member of a laboratory team that will observe each of the stations. The job of each team will be to observe the two substances at each station and determine if the substances are the same or different.

Questions to ask:
1. What is each group trying to determine?
2. How can a group make safe observations?
3. What should group members not do?
4. What should a group do if it can not reach an agreement?

Next:
Discuss a copy of the observation sheet and explain how it should be completed. Divide students into six teams. Give one member of each team an observation sheet and a pencil.

Step Four:
Observing

What to do:
Position one group at each station and let the observations begin. As the children are working, circulate around the stations. Provide plenty of praise for groups that work well together and utilize careful observation techniques. Allow sufficient time for each group to complete its assigned task; then clap your hands and rotate each team to its next activity along a predetermined route. Continue in this manner until each team has visited every station.

Step Five:
Debriefing

What to do:
Gather students together and appoint a spokesperson from each group. Then, beginning with Station One, have each spokesperson report his or her group's findings. Encourage discussion among the members of the groups. Next discuss how real space scientists use similar observation skills to study samples collected in space. While older students will realize that the samples they observed were not really gathered from outer space, younger students may need to have this clarified. After your confession, challenge students to guess the true identities of the substances—based on their observations, of course!

Name _____

70

Six Stations From Space

What do you think?	What senses did you use?	What else did you observe?
Station **1** ○ same ○ different	○ sight ○ touch ○ smell ○ hearing	
Station **2** ○ same ○ different	○ sight ○ touch ○ smell ○ hearing	
Station **3** ○ same ○ different	○ sight ○ touch ○ smell ○ hearing	
Station **4** ○ same ○ different	○ sight ○ touch ○ smell ○ hearing	
Station **5** ○ same ○ different	○ sight ○ touch ○ smell ○ hearing	
Station **6** ○ same ○ different	○ sight ○ touch ○ smell ○ hearing	

A Pocketful Of Science

Getting Heart Smart!

February is National Heart Month, making it the perfect month to incorporate heart-related lessons into your science program. Use the following activities and reproducible to keep your students pumped up about the human heart!

ideas by Ann Flagg

Activity 1: Have A Heart

You will need:
red construction-paper heart
reference book containing an illustration of a human heart
cow or sheep heart from a butcher (optional)
one cardboard paper-towel tube for every two students

What to do:
Invite students to tell what they know about their hearts. Display the heart cutout and ask them why it could not be a human heart. Then show students the human heart illustration. Ask students to compare and contrast the two hearts. (To show students the color, size, and texture of an actual heart muscle, obtain a cow or sheep heart from a butcher.) Next ask each child to make a fist and place it over her heart. Show students the correct location of the heart by positioning your fist in the center of your chest. Explain that a person's heart is about the size of his or her fist. Finally show students how to listen to someone else's heart using a cardboard tube. To do this, place one end of a cardboard tube over a student's heart and listen through the opposite end of the tube. Pair the youngsters, distribute the cardboard tubes, and have students take turns listening to their partners' hearts.

Questions to ask:
1. How is a human heart different from a valentine heart?
2. How do you know that your heart is working?
3. What did you hear when you listened to your partner's heart?
4. What does a doctor use to listen to a heartbeat?

This is why:

The human heart is a hollow, muscular organ that lies near the middle of the chest, between the lungs. The lower region of the heart points toward the left side of the body. Because the beating, or pumping, takes place in this lower region, a child can mistakenly conclude that her entire heart is on the left side of her body. The beating sound of a heart is caused by the closing of the valves inside the heart as the heart allows blood to flow in and out. When a doctor uses a stethoscope to listen to a heart, he hears the "lub dub" sound of the heartbeat.

Activity 2: The Beat Goes On!

You will need:
a half-sheet of scrap paper for each student
clock with a second hand

What to do:
During one minute a child's heart beats approximately 90 times. To help students gain an appreciation for the strength and endurance of their heart muscles, have each student crumple a half-sheet of scrap paper and hold it in one hand. Demonstrate how to make a fist around the paper, and how to squeeze and release the paper without opening your fist. During the next minute count to 90 in a loud voice. Instruct students to firmly squeeze their wads of paper each time you say a number.

Questions to ask:
1. How did the muscles in your hand feel after squeezing the paper 90 times?
2. Does your heart muscle ever stop and rest? How do you know?

This is why:

The heart is a strong pump that continually moves blood through the body. A baby's heart begins beating about eight months before the baby is born, and it continues beating throughout the person's life. In a 70-year lifetime, an average heart pumps about 51 million gallons of blood and beats over two-and-a-half billion times. The only natural rest a heart muscle ever experiences is the brief pause between beats.

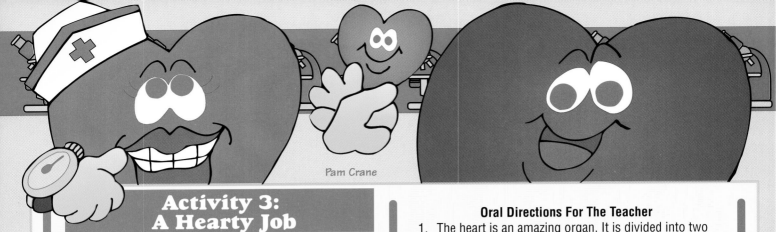

Pam Crane

Activity 3: A Hearty Job

What to do:

Help students understand how a body's heart and circulatory system react to their body's needs. Begin by having each student locate his pulse in his neck or wrist, providing assistance as needed. Ask the students to describe how their pulses feel. Next instruct the students to run in place. After several seconds stop the students and ask them to relocate their pulses.

Questions to ask:

1. How did your pulse and heartbeat change after you ran in place?
2. What kinds of activities would make your heart pump rapidly?
3. When do you think your heart beats the slowest?

This is why:

Oxygen- and nutrient-rich blood travels away from the heart through thick muscular tubes called arteries. In the places where these arteries are close to the skin, a pulse can be felt. When children feel a pulse in their necks or wrists, they are actually feeling the blood being pumped through their bodies' arteries. A person's heart rate is automatically controlled by his nervous system. Since additional activity or anxiety increases a body's need for oxygen, the rate of blood flowing to the heart automatically increases when the person is exercising. Because a resting body requires less oxygen, the rate of blood flowing to a person's heart decreases when he is resting.

Activity 4: An Inside Look

Each student will need:

a copy of page 73   red and blue crayons

What to do:

Give each student a copy of the heart diagram on page 73. Provide the following information and directions for completing the heart activity. (Students may be confused when they discover that *right* and *left* appear to be shown incorrectly on their papers. Clear up this confusion by having each student temporarily place his paper against his chest so he can look down on the heart diagram. Explain that this is the correct position of the heart. Point out that in this position, the right side of the heart is on the right side of the body.)

Oral Directions For The Teacher

1. The heart is an amazing organ. It is divided into two pumps. Each pump is divided into two chambers or spaces. The top chamber on the right side of the heart is called the *right atrium*. Draw a blue box around this name. The lower chamber on the right side of the heart is called the *right ventricle*. Draw a blue box around this name. The top chamber on the left side of the heart is called the *left atrium*. Draw a red box around this name. The lower chamber on the left side of the heart is called the *left ventricle*. Draw a red box around this name.
2. Color the star on your paper blue. This is where blood enters the heart. The blood flows into the right atrium and then into the right ventricle. Then the heart pumps the blood into tubes that take it to the lungs for a fresh supply of oxygen. Use a blue crayon to color the arrows that show this path.
3. Now color the diamond on your paper red. This is where oxygen-rich blood from the lungs reenters the heart. The blood flows into the left atrium and then into the left ventricle. Then the heart pumps the blood out a large tube. This is where the blood begins its trip to other parts of the body. Use a red crayon to color the arrows that show this path.

Questions to ask:

1. What color on your diagram represents tired blood? Restored blood?
2. Which side of the heart has the harder job?
3. Why is it important to keep your heart in good shape?

This is why:

The muscular heart organ is divided into two sides or pumps. Deoxygenated blood, indicated by the blue arrows, enters the right side of the heart through the body's veins and is pumped into the lungs. In the lungs the blood becomes oxygenated (shown as red) and reenters the heart through its left side from which it is then pumped back into the body. The left side of the heart muscle is a bigger and stronger pump because it must push blood through the entire body. It takes about 23 seconds for the heart to circulate blood through the body.

An Inside Look

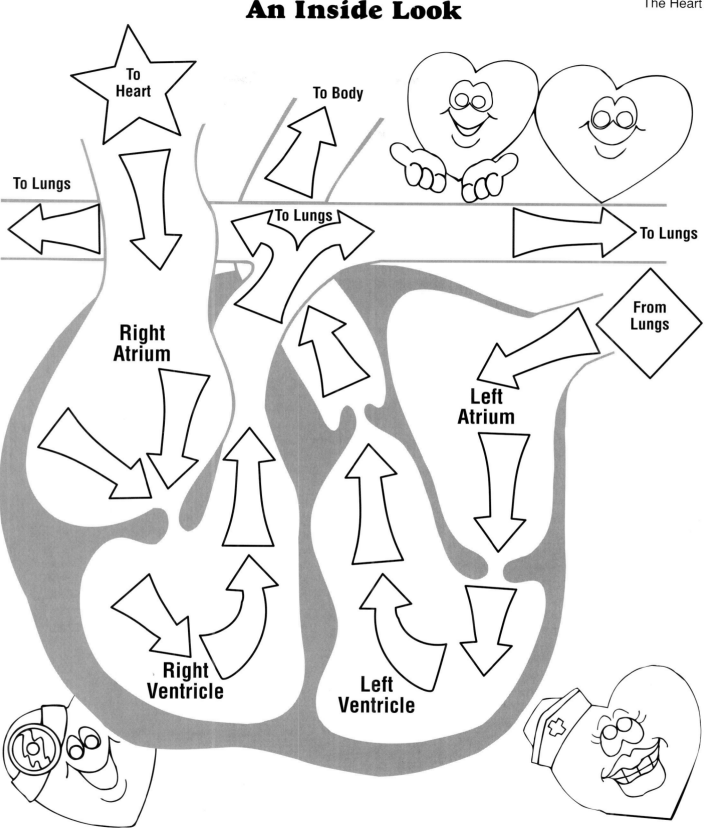

Bonus Box: Your heart is a very important muscle. On the back of this sheet, list three tips for keeping your heart healthy.

An Inside Look At
The Human Body

Enhance your study of the human body with this assortment of activities, experiments, resources, and reproducibles.

Sherlock Bones
B.I.
(Body Investigator)

Getting Started

Begin your human body study in a big way! Each youngster needs a length of butcher paper large enough to draw his body shape on. Then, working in pairs, have each student take a turn lying on his length of paper while his partner traces his shape onto the paper. Next have each youngster color one side of his cutout to resemble himself (fully clothed) before cutting it out. As youngsters are coloring, have them brainstorm similarities between their bodies. If students become stumped, encourage them to think about what is inside each of their bodies. What a great place to begin your study of the human body!

Later have students draw and color their body organs on the backs of their cutouts. Or divide students into small groups and have each group illustrate a different body system.

Locating Resources

Many resources are available for teaching about the human body. The following two resources (each with a related activity) are a great place to begin your search for information. On the following pages, you will also find additional resources for specific topics such as digestion, blood, and muscles.

The Magic School Bus Inside The Human Body
Written by Joanna Cole
Published by Scholastic Inc.

Ms. Frizzle's students are used to her rather unusual teaching methods, but they're not prepared for what happens when they take a class field trip to the local science museum. Instead of viewing a museum exhibit, the busload of students is swallowed by a classmate. Once inside the student's body, Ms. Frizzle takes the group on a guided tour, demonstrating the inner workings of the digestive system, bloodstream, brain, and nervous system. What better way to get an inside look at the human body!

Point out the student reports that are featured on several pages of the book. Then, using the pattern and directions on page 78, have each student make a bus booklet. Throughout your study of the human body, challenge students to fill the pages of their books with fascinating facts, and questions and answers about the human body.

What Am I Made Of?
Written by David Bennett
Published by Aladdin Books

Get the basics from this delightful book. Simple text and animated illustrations provide an elementary introduction to the workings of the human body, skeletons, skin, circulation, and nervous system. At the completion of the book, have each student sit motionless for 30 seconds and think about what is going on inside his body. Then invite students to share their thoughts. Gosh, it's hard work sitting still!

Can You Swallow This?

Incorporate these activities and resources into your study of the digestive system.

Down The Tube!

Introduce the digestive system with this eye-opening demonstration. Cut a 32-foot length of adding machine tape. (This is the approximate length of a person's digestive tract.) At one end of the tape, write the following sentence: "The digestive system is a long muscular tube that runs through the body. This tube is about 32 feet long." Place the length of tape inside a desk drawer, making sure that the unprogrammed end is easily accessible. Invite students to share what they know about the digestive system. When appropriate, explain that you also have a couple of facts to share. Begin to pull the length of tape from the drawer and continue until the entire tape is exposed. Then read the facts written on the tape. Without a doubt you'll have captured your youngsters' attention and intrigued their curiosity about the digestive system.

Use the same tape for a fun review activity. Extend the tape in an open area. Then, on the tape, have students write the things that they have learned about the digestive tract. Or cut the tape into several shorter lengths (one per student) and complete a similar activity.

Do Not Enter!

This simple experiment helps youngsters understand how food molecules pass through the walls of the small intestine and into the bloodstream.

What you need:

coffee filter	one tsp. sugar
spoon	two clear glasses
one tsp. cocoa	water

What to do:

Push your fingers into the center of the coffee filter to make a funnel shape; then place the filter in a clear glass as shown. Fill the second glass about one-fourth full of water; then add the sugar and cocoa. Stir until the sugar and cocoa are completely mixed into the water. Holding the filter in place, slowly pour the liquid mixture into the filter; then allow the mixture to drip into the bottom of the glass.

What happens?

The filter traps the particles of cocoa and prevents them from passing through the tiny openings in the paper. The sugar and water, however, easily pass through the paper. This same process happens inside the body.

Digested food passes through the walls of the *small intestine* in order to reach the cells of your body. But other large substances, such as waste particles, are kept out. These larger particles move into the *large intestine*.

What Happens To A Hamburger

Get to the meat of the digestive system with this delightful Reading Rainbow book (published by Harper Trophy). In an easy-to-read fashion, author Paul Showers explains the processes by which a hamburger and other foods pass through all of the parts of the digestive system. The end result: strong bones, solid muscles, and lots of energy!

Totally Cellular

Incorporate these activities and resources into your study of the circulatory system.

You Can't Live Without It!

Paul Showers's book entitled *A Drop Of Blood* (published by Thomas Y. Crowell) presents a simple and delightfully illustrated introduction to the composition and functions of blood. For added fun, have students bring flashlights to school on the day that you plan to read the book aloud. Then have students use their flashlights to complete the simple activities included in the book. That's my blood!

Round And Round And Round

In less than one minute, a person's blood circulates or makes a trip through his body. There are three basic kinds of vessels that carry blood, and each kind has a special job or function.

- Blood rushes away from the heart through *arteries*. Arteries are large tubes with thick elastic walls. These are the vessels that you press for a pulse count.
- *Capillaries* are the tiniest blood vessels. Each capillary is finer than a hair. These tiny vessels filter nutrients into the body's tissues. They also filter waste from the tissues back into the bloodstream.
- *Veins* return blood to the heart and lungs. They appear as blue lines under the skin. Blood flowing through the veins moves very slowly in comparison to blood rushing through the arteries.

To view these vessels, have each youngster use a mirror and a strong light to look at the underside of his tongue. Thick pink lines (arteries) and thick blue lines (veins) can easily be spotted. Capillaries (tiny hair-thin red lines) may be less visible. For a close-up look at capillaries have the student look in the fold under his eye.

Listening In

The rhythmic contracting and relaxing of the heart moves blood through the body. With these student-made stethoscopes, students can listen to their own heartbeats and the heartbeats of others. To make a stethoscope, fit one end of a length of rubber tubing (available from a hardware store) over the small end of a funnel. (To make a funnel, simply cut away the bottom portion of a plastic two-liter soda bottle.) Place the open end of the funnel over the heart and the unattached end of the rubber hose to your ear. Lub-DUB—lub-DUB—lub-Dub…

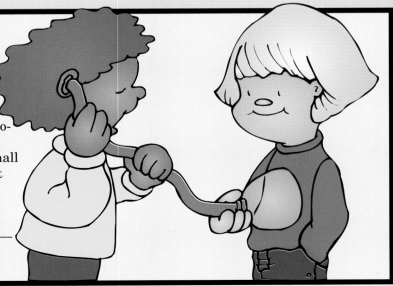

Making A Move

Incorporate these activities and resources into your study of the muscular system.

A Whole Lot Of Muscle!

The human body has over 600 major muscles. For a fun cooperative-learning activity, give each group of students a large container and a supply of shaped pasta, dried beans, or other manipulatives. Challenge the students in each group to count 600 manipulatives into its container. When the collections are complete, have each group remove a set of 34 manipulatives (muscles) from its container and a set of 13. Explain that each set represents the muscles needed to complete one movement. Invite students to guess the identities of the movements before revealing that it takes 34 muscles to frown and 13 to smile!

Pick A Move

Warm up your youngsters' muscles with this fun-filled movement game. To begin, pair students and have each student face his partner. To start the game, one student in the pair makes a move; then his partner repeats the move and adds a move of his own. Play continues back and forth between the partners in this manner until one player forgets a move from the sequence or repeats a move in the wrong order. Once students are familiar with the game, have each twosome join another twosome; then begin a new round of play. A player is out of the game when he makes an incorrect move. Encourage youngsters to use a variety of moves, using muscles from their heads to their toes!

Dinosaurs Alive And Well A Guide To Good Health
Written and Illustrated by Laurie Krasny Brown and Marc Brown
Published by Little, Brown and Company

This entertaining book is packed with good advice on topics such as exercising your body and your mind, good nutrition, and family relationships. Being healthy has never seemed more fun!

At the completion of the book, have students brainstorm healthful habits as you list their ideas on the chalkboard. Then, working individually or in pairs, have students design wellness posters to be displayed around the school. Through their posters, youngsters can encourage other students to take active roles in their physical and emotional well-being.

Pattern

Name _____

Note To Teacher: Use the pattern with *The Magic School Bus...* on page 74. Duplicate student copies of the pattern on yellow construction paper. Provide a supply of 5" x 7" blank paper. To make a front cover, a student creates a likeness of himself in the large bus window by using construction-paper scraps, markers, or crayons. If desired, he creates additional passengers in the remaining bus windows and colors in desired details. Next he writes his name and a title on the bus before he cuts the pattern out. To make a back cover, the student traces his front cover onto a 9" x 12" sheet of yellow construction paper and cuts on the resulting outline. To complete his booklet, the student staples a predetermined number of blank paper sheets between his two covers.

Rockhound Readiness

An Introduction To Rocks

Polish your students' observation, description, classification, and scientific thinking skills using these hands-on, rock-related activities and reproducibles. You won't need to be a rockhound to discover that this unit is a real gem!

ideas by Bill O'Connor

Digging In

Dig into your study of rocks by asking each student to collect and bring to school five to ten different rocks. Each rock should be larger than a quarter, but smaller than the student's fist. Accept all rocks, even those that have not occurred naturally (such as concrete, pottery, blacktop, and plaster). These rocks can be distinguished later. Discourage students from bringing labeled rock collections. These collections will be more useful and interesting at the conclusion of the unit.

Scrub A Dub

Use this activity to hone your students' observation skills. Ask students to predict how their rocks will change when they are washed. After some discussion, have each student wash his rocks using water and a small brush or toothbrush. Discuss the changes students observe. (Rocks may or may not show visual changes. Some rocks may absorb the water, give off unusual odors, or even disintegrate.) When the rocks have dried, have students decide if the changes observed were permanent or temporary.

Rock Talk

Create a "quarry" of descriptive rock words during this brainstorming activity. Divide a large sheet of bulletin board paper into four columns. Entitle the columns *color, texture, luster,* and *shape.* Discuss the meaning of each column title, defining *texture* as the way a rock feels and *luster* as the way a rock "shines" in the light. Then have students brainstorm descriptive rock words for each category. Write the words on the chart. Make additions to this "word quarry" throughout your rock study.

Our Word Quarry

Color	Texture	Luster	Shape
black red orange white stripes	grainy jagged rough smooth slick	shiny dull sparkly metallic flat	flat round square oval

Mystery Rocks

Continue to sharpen your students' observation skills with this rock guessing game. Select one rock from each student's collection. Display the resulting rock collection so it can easily be viewed. Tell students you are thinking of one rock in the collection. Then challenge students to determine the rock's identity by asking questions that can be answered with yes or no responses. Encourage students to refer to the "word quarry" (see "Rock Talk") for descriptive words. Let the student who correctly identifies the mystery rock secretly select another rock from the collection and respond to his classmates' questions.

Grouping Rocks

Here's an activity that will activate your students' observation and classification skills. Use the rock collection from "Mystery Rocks" or create one in a similar manner. Working in teams, have students decide which rocks in the collection "belong together." Have the teams take turns sorting the rocks atop a sheet of laminated poster board. Have one team member use a wipe-off marker to label each grouping. Accept all groupings that are based on observable physical properties. Wipe away the programming before the next group takes its turn.

Next challenge each student to group his own rock collection in a similar manner. Or have each team of students combine their collections and group the resulting collection. Debates and disagreements can easily surface during this type of an activity. Remind students that rocks can be correctly grouped in a variety of ways. Make it a point to praise teams which are working together cooperatively.

Beyond The Observable
Dig into these rock tests and uncover more rock revelations!

The Streak Test: This test reveals the true colors of rocks. Have students stroke each of their rocks on the back of household ceramic tile, atop an unglazed porcelain tile, or on a concrete sidewalk. Group together those rocks which leave the same colors of streaks. If applicable, also form a group of rocks which leave no streaks. Explain that the true color of a rock may be discolored by environmental factors. The resulting streak of each rock reveals its true color. If a streak is not made, this indicates that the rock is harder than the tile or concrete. A rock will only leave a streak when it is stroked against a surface which is harder than the rock itself.

The Hardness Test: This test demonstrates the hardness of rocks. A student will use his fingernail, a penny, a table knife or steel file, a small glass pane, and the criteria shown to determine the hardness of each of his rocks. (For safety purposes, adhere the glass pane to a tabletop by covering the rough edges with durable tape.)

A *very soft rock* can be scratched by a fingernail.

A *soft rock* can be scratched by a penny, but not by a fingernail.

A *medium rock* will scratch a penny, but it will not scratch a table knife or a steel file.

A *hard rock* will scratch a table knife or a steel file, but it will not scratch the glass.

A *very hard rock* will scratch the glass.

Have students group their rocks based on their test results, then order the rocks by hardness. If the above materials cannot be obtained, have students try to order their rocks by stroking the rocks against each other. Remind students that a rock which makes a scratch is the harder rock.

The Acid Test: Use this test to group rocks in yet another way. Place a few drops of vinegar on each rock. Group together rocks which react to the vinegar and rocks which do not. Explain that rocks which contain the mineral *carbonate* (such as limestone and marble) will cause the vinegar to bubble or fizz.

The Matter Of Mass

Have students determine the comparative mass of each rock in their collections by lifting the rocks and comparing their weights. Then have each student attempt to order his rocks from the least to the most massive. Point out that the size of a rock cannot determine its weight. To prove this, have each student pair two rocks to demonstrate that a smaller rock can outweigh a larger rock.

Taking A Peek Inside

To take a peek at the inside surfaces of a rock, first wrap the rock in several layers of newspaper before placing it inside a paper bag. Don a pair of safety glasses; then place the bag on a durable surface. Strike the packaged rock with a hammer until it breaks apart. Unwrap and display the broken rock. Explain that rocks break apart in one of two ways, depending on their compositions. A breakage may result in smooth flat surfaces *(cleavage)* or rough, irregular surfaces *(fracture)*. Have students identify the type of breakage. Then have students compare the color and texture of the rock's inside surfaces to its outside surfaces. Ask students to give reasons why the inside and outside surfaces of a rock often differ.

Honorable Rockhounds

Appoint your students "honorable rockhounds" and challenge them to showcase their rock knowledge with this hands-on activity. Duplicate student copies of pages 82 and 83. To make a booklet, complete the title page; then cut on the dotted lines and stack the resulting pages so the title page is on top of the stack. Color and cut out the booklet covers; then staple the pages between the covers. Have each student choose a favorite rock from his collection, then complete his booklet pages by observing and testing the rock.

To extend the activity, collect the completed booklets and their corresponding rocks. Redistribute the booklets, making certain each student receives a booklet other than his own. Place the rocks at a center. In turn, have small groups of students take these booklets to the center and try to determine which rocks correspond to the booklets. Have each student verify his choice with the student who completed the booklet.

Looking Ahead

At the completion of these activities, students will be eager to learn more about rocks. Filmstrips, labeled rock and mineral collections, a visit to a science museum, or a visiting mineralogist or geologist (professional or amateur) would all be appropriate and educational. And for an unusual adventure, hop aboard a magic school bus and travel inside the earth. The book *The Magic School Bus Inside The Earth,* by Joanna Cole, provides a lesson in geology that is totally motivating, informative, and unforgettable!

A Rock Review

written by

The Honorable
Rockhound

_____

Where was the rock found?

_____

_____

_____

What color is the rock?

_____

_____

_____

How does the rock feel when you touch it? _____

_____

_____

_____

Tell about the shape of the rock.

_____

_____

_____

How does the rock look when you hold it near a light? _____

_____

_____

_____

Did the rock leave a streak?

_____

If it did, what color was the streak?

_____

Tell about the mass of the rock.

_____

_____

_____

©1997 The Education Center, Inc. • *The Best Of* The Mailbox® *Science • Primary •* TEC836

82   **Note To Teacher:** Use with "Honorable Rockhounds" on page 81.

Tell about the hardness of the rock.

_____

_____

_____

Describe one special thing about the rock. _____

_____

_____

_____

Booklet Covers

©1997 The Education Center, Inc. • TEC836

Completed Booklet

©1997 The Education Center, Inc. • *The Best Of* The Mailbox® *Science* • *Primary* • TEC836

Note To Teacher: Use with "Honorable Rockhounds" on page 81.

83

SHIMMY-SHIMMY

Earthquakes are fascinating—sometimes scary—natural phenomena. Help students understand, respect, and prepare for an earthquake with these upbeat activities and reproducibles. Without a doubt, student response will reach a record high on the Richter scale!

ideas contributed by Chris Christensen

Rumble, Rumble, Tumble

What happens during an earthquake? How does an earthquake feel? What causes an earthquake? Students will be filled with earthquake questions such as these. After students have shared their questions and experiences, explain that an earthquake is the sudden, rapid shaking of the earth. Demonstrate an earthquake by placing a box partially filled with soil on top of a desk. Inside the box, pile small paper containers (plates, cups, boxes) one on top of the other to create several tall structures. Gently shake the box until the structures topple. Students should conclude that the shaking of the earth (the soil-filled box) can cause structures to fall.

Earthquakes Of Long Ago

Earthquakes have been happening for many, many years, but scientists have only been studying earthquakes with scientific instruments for a short time. Because people didn't know why earthquakes happened, they created stories or legends to explain them. Students will enjoy writing and illustrating their own earthquake legends. Share the following legends as a pre-writing activity. Be sure to provide time for student volunteers to share their own earthshaking creations!

- Long ago in Greece, people believed the earth was balanced on the shoulders of the Greek god, Atlas. Each time Atlas shifted the earth from one shoulder to the other an earthquake occurred.
- Long ago in India, people believed the earth was balanced on the head of an elephant that sat on the back of a tortoise. If either animal moved, the earth shook.
- Long ago in Russia, people believed a giant god rode across the ice fields on a dogsled. When the dogs pulling the sled stopped to scratch their fleas the earth trembled.

The Earth's Layers

Take a peek inside the earth by comparing it to a hard-boiled egg. The outer layer of the earth (the *crust*) is something like the egg shell, the middle layer (the *mantle*) is something like the egg white, and the inside layer (the *core*) is something like the egg yolk. Slice the egg (shell and all) to show the layers. Share the following facts; then have students complete duplicated copies of "Layers Of The Earth" on page 87.

- **The crust** is a hard, rocky layer. It is very thin compared to the other layers of the earth.

- **The mantle** is mostly solid rock.
- **The core** is like a hot ball. It helps to heat the earth.

SHAKE! An Introduction To Earthquakes

A Giant Puzzle

Who would guess that the crust of the earth is divided into sections called *plates?* These plates fit together like a jigsaw puzzle. To reinforce this concept, enlarge (if desired) and duplicate the map on page 87 onto white construction paper. Have students color the shaded areas (land) brown and the unshaded areas (water) blue, before cutting on the bold lines. Then have each student re-create the flattened representation of the earth by arranging and gluing his puzzle pieces (plates) on another piece of paper. Inform students that most experts agree the earth's crust is divided into seven to twelve major plates and a number of smaller ones.

On The Move

Learn more about the earth's layers with this activity. In an open area, cluster three students with their backs together to represent the earth's core. Have these students pretend to be very hot by wiping their brows and fanning themselves. For the mantle, direct 12 students to stand in groups of three around the core. Have each group move together in a slow, circular motion. Have the remaining students represent the crust by loosely joining hands and forming a circle facing the mantle. Instruct these students to gently sway in unison from side to side. After a short amount of time, stop the motion and ask students what they have learned about the earth's layers. Students should conclude that there is heat and movement within the earth. Explain that the movement of the plates is a constant motion, while the unpredictable movement inside the earth represents trapped energy.

Earthquake!

To roughly demonstrate how an earthquake occurs, have students resume their positions from "On The Move." Once students are in motion, instruct one mantle group to gently bump (or release energy) into the crust, causing its students to bump against each other. Explain that the transfer of energy from the mantle to the crust caused the plates to bump into each other, causing an earthquake. An earthquake can also occur when the earth's plates move away from each other or grind past each other.

Our Shapely Earth

While examining a relief map or globe, ask students to imagine an earth without mountains, valleys, and plateaus—a flat earth. Now that's pretty boring! Point out to students that it has been earth-moving events such as earthquakes that have helped give our earth its beautiful shapes. Over billions of years the changes which occur during earthquakes can become very significant!

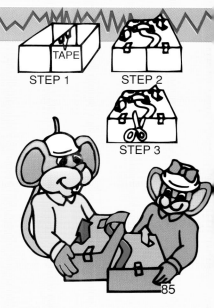

STEP 1
STEP 2
STEP 3

Learning About Faults

Earthquake movement can also occur at cracks in the earth's plates called *faults.* Brainstorm a list of things found in a country setting such as trees, fences, roads, fields, rivers, bridges, and houses. (Do not include people or animals.) Have student pairs refer to the list as they construct country settings on 9" x 12" sheets of construction paper using crayons, markers, construction paper scraps, and glue.

To simulate a fault, have each pair tape together two shoe boxes (Step 1), then securely tape its project over the joined boxes, trimming the project if necessary (Step 2). Tear or cut the project apart at the *fault line* (Step 3); then remove the tape holding the boxes together. To demonstrate an up-and-down fault movement, instruct students to press their boxes together, then release the pressure and let one box drop (or rise) about one inch. To demonstrate a sideways movement, press the boxes together; then release the pressure and slide the boxes past each other. Have students examine and describe the effects of each demonstration on their projects.

More Cracks!

Sometimes the *surface* of the earth cracks during an earthquake. Generally these cracks or *fissures* develop near the *epicenter* (the part of the earth's surface directly above the energy source of the earthquake). Here's a tasty way to illustrate fissuring without an earthquake! Fold two cups of whipped topping, one beaten egg, and one teaspoon of vanilla together in a large bowl. Add a boxed cake mix (any flavor) and stir well. Drop by the teaspoonful into one-half cup of powdered sugar, and coat lightly. Place on a lightly greased cookie sheet. Bake at 350 degrees for 18–20 minutes or until lightly browned. (Makes approximately three dozen cookies.) Have students note the fissures in the cookie surfaces, before indulging. Now isn't that a perfect treat for a hardworking student seismologist?

Connie Connely, Tulsa, OK

Stressed-out Rocks!

Earthquakes happen when stored energy is released. When a rock is being squeezed or pulled apart, scientists say the rock is under stress. Rocks try to absorb these stresses by changing their shapes. If the stresses are removed, the rocks return to their original shapes. If the stresses continue, eventually the rocks break. When this happens an earthquake occurs.

To demonstrate similar stress, push on the sides of an inflated balloon. Notice how the balloon shape changes. Release the pressure and the balloon returns to its original shape. Continue the pressure and the balloon eventually pops. Or stretch a rubber band and notice the lengthening of the band. Release the pressure and the band returns to its original shape. Continue pulling on the band and it eventually breaks!

Quakes Of All Sizes

Remind students that an earthquake is caused when energy stored within the earth is released. The amount of energy released determines the strength of the earthquake. The larger the amount of energy released, the stronger the earthquake, and vice versa. Use the same supplies mentioned in "Rumble, Rumble, Tumble" on page 84 to demonstrate this concept. When your structures are built, have a student gently nudge the table. Discuss how this small amount of energy affected the structures. Next have the student nudge the table with a little more force or energy and discuss the results. Continue in this manner until the structures fall. Encourage students to experiment with the forces of energy by creating similar projects at home.

There Is No Warning

Earthquakes can happen anywhere and at any time. And that's a scary thought! Reassure students that, by planning ahead, they can be ready in case an earthquake hits their area. Discuss and complete the worksheet on page 88. Follow up this activity by determining safety spots inside and outside your classroom. Also encourage students to discuss safety spots and prepare earthquake safety kits with their parents.

The Tremor Troop

FEMA and NSTA (National Science Teachers Association) have developed an earthquake curriculum for elementary classroom teachers and their students. Product distribution is limited to one free copy per school while the supply lasts. Call 1-800-480-2520 or send your request on school letterhead to:

FEMA Distribution Warehouse
P.O. Box 2012
Jessup, MD 20794-2012

Layers Of The Earth

Label and color the layers of the earth.
Use the color code.

Color Code	
crust	= green
mantle	= yellow
core	= red

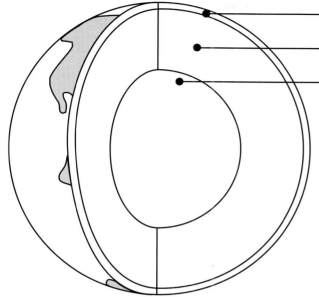

Fill in the blanks.

1. We live on the layer of earth called the

   _____ .

2. The hottest layer of earth is called the

   _____ .

3. The largest layer of earth is called the

   _____ .

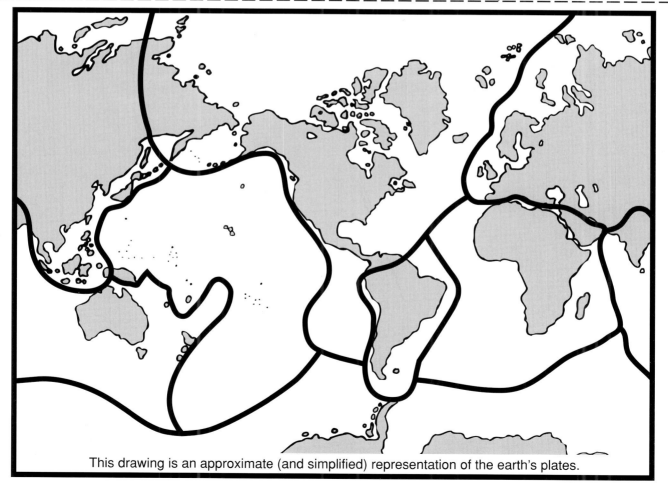

This drawing is an approximate (and simplified) representation of the earth's plates.

Be Prepared!

Which items belong in an earthquake safety kit?
Cut.
Paste.

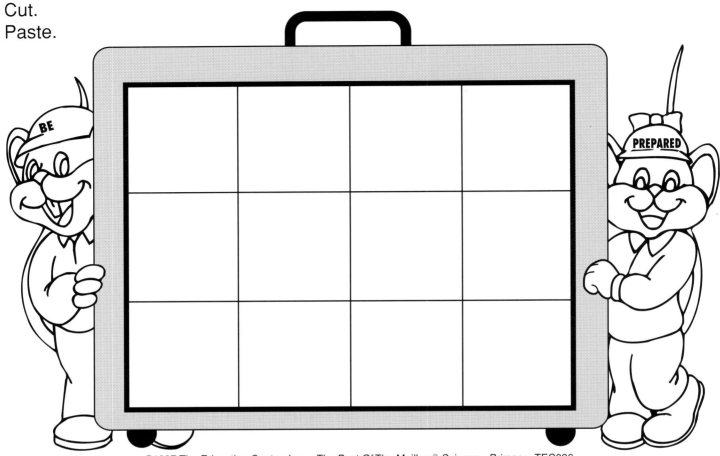

©1997 The Education Center, Inc. • *The Best Of* The Mailbox® *Science* • *Primary* • TEC836

Bonus Box: Glue the pictures you have left on another sheet of paper. Write a sentence or two telling why these items would not be helpful in an earthquake safety kit.

powdered milk	first aid kit	ice cream	blankets	pizza	gloves
flashlight	computer	fire extinguisher	fresh fruit	can opener	batteries
tools	canned food	iron	bottled water	skateboard	portable radio

Note To Teacher: Explain to students that an earthquake safety kit should include items that may be needed after an earthquake if there is no running water and/or electricity.

Wild About Weather!

Here's your chance to do more than just talk about the weather! Dip into this weather-wise collection of hands-on activities and discover a whirlwind of teaching success. And that's a forecast you can count on!

Hats Off To Weather!

Introduce your weather unit with this hats-on approach! In a large shopping bag, place an assortment of hats such as a rain hat, a stocking cap, a straw hat, a baseball cap, and a sun visor. Gather students around you, then remove one hat from the bag and place it on your head. Ask students to describe what the weather might be if a person chose to wear this hat. Retrieve another hat from the bag and place it on the head of a youngster. Ask students to describe the type(s) of weather this hat might be worn in. Continue in this manner until all of the hats are being worn. Ask students if they think weather forecasters or meteorologists predict the weather by observing the hats that people wear. Record your youngsters' thoughts about how weather is predicted on a large raindrop cutout and display the cutout for future reference. Then collect the hats and start observing the weather!

Paula L. Diekhoff, Warsaw, IN

Background For The Teacher

Weather is the condition of the air that blankets our earth. It is shaped by four "ingredients": the sun, the earth, the air, and water. These ingredients work together to make it hot or cold, cloudy or clear, windy or calm. They may produce rain, snow, sleet, or hail.

One universal aspect of weather is that it affects everyone. The type of clothing that we wear each day, how we spend our leisure time, and even our moods are tied into the weather. Weather also has a tremendous impact on farming, industry, transportation, communication, construction, and sometimes, our very survival.

A Writing Forecast

Your youngsters' writing skills can weather any storm with this colossal collection of journal writing topics. For added writing motivation, have each youngster design his own theme-shaped writing journal!

- Lost In The Fog
- The Raindrop That Was Afraid To Fall
- The Day There Was No Weather
- The Little Lost Cloud
- Trapped Inside A Raindrop!
- My Pet Tornado
- Silly Snow
- The Day It Rained Bats And Frogs
- The Wind That Was A Bully
- The Unforgettable Forecast

A Flurry Of Creative Expression

Many people believe that weather affects the behavior of animals and humans. Give your youngsters an opportunity to express their creative interpretations of different types of weather. If desired, play a recording of classical background music and have each youngster hold a crepe-paper streamer as she moves around the room, interpreting various weather conditions such as a cold wind, a thunderstorm, a hurricane, a flurry of snowflakes, a bolt of lightning, a gusty wind, a downpour of rain, a warm spring breeze, and a sunny day. Be sure to join in on the fun yourself!

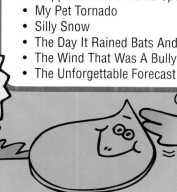

Reading Thermometers

This quick and easy activity gives youngsters firsthand experience reading thermometers. Divide students into small groups and give each group an ice cube in a cup of cold water and an outdoor thermometer. Select one student in each group to hold the bulb of the thermometer between her fingers. This will cause the liquid in the thermometer to rise. Then ask the student to insert the bulb of the thermometer into the cup of water, causing the liquid in the thermometer to drop. Ask students to share their observations. Explain that holding the bulb of the thermometer increases the temperature of the liquid inside the thermometer. As the liquid is heated, it expands and rises in the thermometer tube. The cold water removes the heat from the liquid in the thermometer. When the liquid cools, it contracts and moves down the tube. Thermometers measure the temperature of air in the same way. Any increase or decrease in the heat content of air causes the liquid inside the thermometer to expand or contract. Now that students fully understand how a thermometer works, they'll enjoy monitoring the temperature of the air outside your classroom.

Clouds! Clouds! Clouds!

For an interesting and informative look at the different types of clouds and the weather that follows them, share *The Cloud Book* by Tomie dePaola (published by Holiday House) with your youngsters. At the completion of the book, write a student-generated list of cloud types on a large cloud cutout. If desired, write a brief description of each cloud type near its name. Then for each of several days, schedule a few minutes of sky-watching into your weather activities. Conclude each session by discussing the cloud types that were observed. As an added challenge, ask students to predict the weather conditions that will follow each cloud type.

When students are familiar with a variety of cloud types, have them create fold-out cloud booklets. To make a booklet, accordion-fold a 5" x 3' strip of blue bulletin-board paper to create a booklet that is approximately five inches square. On the front of the booklet, write your name and the booklet's title. On the bottom half of each booklet page, name and describe a different type of cloud. Then on the top half of the pages, create resemblances of the clouds using cotton balls, crayons, and glue.

It was so hot that Frederick wore his snowsuit to school.

How Weather-Wise Are You?

Thinking caps are a must for this weather-related challenge! Duplicate student copies of the activity on page 94. Have students search for the misused weather words independently or in pairs. After the words have been found and replaced, check the activity together.

For a fun follow-up activity, create a book of similar weather-teasers. To make a booklet page, have each child fold a blank 8 1/2" x 11" sheet of paper in half. Making certain that the fold is at the bottom of his paper, the youngster writes and illustrates a weather sentence containing a misused weather word. Next he flips his paper over so that the fold is at the top. Then he writes and illustrates the correct version of the sentence. Mount these papers on colorful sheets of 9" x 12" construction paper that have been folded in half. (See illustration.) Bind the booklet pages between a booklet cover entitled "How Weather-Wise Are You?" The completed booklet is sure to create a flurry of reading excitement!

Paula L. Diekhoff, Warsaw, IN

In A Fog About Fog

So what is fog anyway? Undoubtedly your youngsters will have a few ideas of their own. After students have had a chance to share their explanations, reveal that fog is actually a cloud that touches the ground. To make fog in a bottle, gather the following materials: a cup of hot water, a clear gallon jug, matches, a basketball or bicycle tire pump, and modeling clay.

Pour the cup of hot water into the bottle. Light a match, blow it out, and drop it into the bottle. Quickly seal the opening of the bottle with clay, leaving a small opening for inserting the air pump tube. Pump up the pressure inside the jar with about 15 to 20 strokes. Then remove the air pump, releasing the pressure. The air inside the bottle will instantly turn to fog! If you pump up the pressure again, the air will clear.

Why does it work? Increasing the air pressure warms the air inside the jar, allowing it to hold more water vapor. When the pressure is suddenly reduced, the water condenses into tiny droplets that produce fog. The smoke particles represent the dust particles that are present in the atmosphere.

Homemade Weather Instruments

While commercially made weather instruments provide the most reliable results, home-made instruments are fun for kids to make, and they help illustrate weather concepts just as well. We think you'll find these easy-to-make projects perfect for your weather studies.

ideas by Mary Beth Rollick

Barometer

Air pressure is measured with an instrument called a barometer.

Materials: plastic container, balloon, rubber band, drinking straw, tape, poster board, marker, ruler

How to make and use: Cut a small piece of balloon and stretch it over the top of the container. Use the rubber band to secure the balloon in place. Tape the straw to the middle of the balloon as shown. Fold a piece of poster board so that it is self-standing. Position the poster board next to the straw and mark where the straw intersects the poster board. Then use the ruler to create a scale from 0 to 10 on the poster board. Design the scale so that the original point of intersection is at 5. Position the barometer and the scale side by side, taping the scale in place, if desired. Check the barometer at the same time each day and note where the straw intersects the scale. Changes in the air pressure will cause the balloon and the straw to move slightly upward or downward.

Rain Gauge

A rain gauge measures the amount of rain that falls.

Materials: empty 2-liter plastic bottle, scissors or knife, permanent marker, wooden stake, large rubber bands, hammer

How to make and use: Remove the top third of the plastic bottle, then invert the top inside the bottom forming a funnel. Use the marker to make a desired scale on the side of the bottle. Drive the stake into level ground in an open area. Set the bottle beside the stake, then use the rubber bands to secure the bottle to the stake. (This will keep the rain gauge upright.) Take daily readings of the amount of rainfall. Each time you record a measurement, remember to pour out the rainwater.

Anemometer

Wind strength is measured by an instrument called an anemometer.

Materials: 3 small yogurt containers, 3 knitting needles, large cork, broomstick, hammer, nail (must be longer that the cork), 2 washers, stopwatch

How to make and use: Spray paint one yogurt container a bright color. Make two holes on opposite sides of each yogurt container, 1 1/4 inches from the top. Push a knitting needle through the holes in each container, then push the needles into the sides of the cork so that they are equally spaced around it. Make a hole through the center of the cork and push the nail completely through the cork. Put the washers on the end of the nail, then hammer the nail into the top of the broomstick so that the cork can spin around easily. Find an open space outside and stick the broomstick in the ground. When the wind blows, the anemometer will spin around. To check the wind speed, count the number of times the painted container passes by you in ten seconds. The higher the number, the stronger the wind.

Wind Direction Finder

A wind direction finder (also called a weather vane or wind vane) shows the direction the wind is blowing from.

Materials: poster board, scissors, tape, pen top, knitting needle, modeling clay, brick, marker, white contact paper (or other adhesive paper), compass

How to make and use: Cut an arrow from the poster board and tape a pen top to its middle. Press a tiny lump of clay to the arrow point as shown. Use the remaining clay to affix the knitting needle to the brick, then slide the pen top over the needle. Cut out four squares of adhesive paper and write one of the following letters on each square: N (north), S (south), E (east), W (west). Take the squares, the compass, and the wind vane outdoors. Position the vane in a large open area. (The higher the vane, the better the reading.) Then using the compass as a reference, attach the directional labels to the sides of the brick. Observe the arrow several times a day. Remember that the arrow will point in the direction that the wind is blowing *from*.

Oh, The Weather Outside Is...

sunny overcast cloudy hazy frosty
cool stormy clear freezing wet
breezy chilly foggy fair hot
windy humid blustery cold rainy

Write each word in a raindrop.
Then use the code to **outline** each raindrop.

Color Code

blue = I like this kind of weather.
black = I do not like this kind of weather.
purple = I'm not sure how I feel about this kind of weather.

Bonus Box: On the back of this sheet, list three ways that the weather affects what you do during a normal day.

Name _____

Just The Facts, Please!

Decide if each sentence is a **fact** or an **opinion**.
Cut out the strips.
Glue the strips on the weather chart.

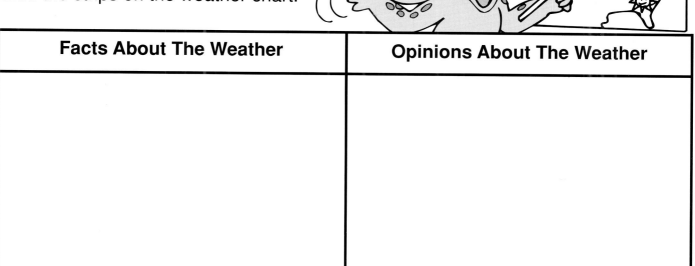

Facts About The Weather	Opinions About The Weather

Bonus Box: What do you think is the best thing about studying the weather? Write your opinion on the back of this sheet.

Everyone feels sad when it rains.	Summer weather is the best weather.
Lightning is very dangerous.	Water evaporates more quickly in the sun.
A foggy night is scary.	A tornado can cause a lot of damage.
Snowflakes are beautiful.	Forecasting the weather is fun.
The weather affects how people dress.	There are many different kinds of clouds.

Name _____

Weather Bloopers

How weather-wise are you?
Cross out the weather word in each sentence
   that doesn't make sense.
Write the correct weather word in the cloud.
Use the answer bank.

1. A prediction about the weather is called a weather observation.

2. The atmosphere warms the earth.

3. During a storm you might see lightning and hear snowflakes.

4. When water freezes, it changes to fog.

5. Cirrus, stratus, and cumulus are types of frost.

6. A thermometer is an instrument for measuring rainfall.

7. Moving air is called snow.

8. A person who studies weather is called a barometer.

9. Hail is a cloud that touches the ground.

10. After the rain shower a colorful hurricane filled the sky.

11. Water freezes more rapidly in the sun.

12. Sleet, wind, hail, and snow are all kinds of precipitation.

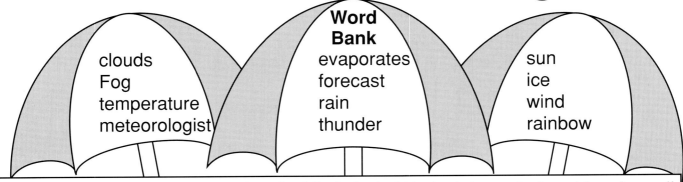

Word Bank

clouds	evaporates	sun
Fog	forecast	ice
temperature	rain	wind
meteorologist	thunder	rainbow

Bonus Box: What is your favorite kind of weather? On the back of this sheet, draw and color a picture of yourself doing what you like to do most in your favorite kind of weather.

©1997 The Education Center, Inc. • *The Best Of* The Mailbox® *Science • Primary* • TEC836 • Key p. 159

Note To Teacher: Use this activity with "How Weather-Wise Are You?" on page 90.

A Literary Forecast

Use this collection of books and related activities to enhance your weather unit.

books reviewed by Deborah Zink Roffino

Weather And Climate

Written by Barbara Taylor
Published by Kingfisher Books

Discovery and experimentation fill this easy-to-follow overview of the earth's weather. Inviting projects for class or individual work such as making a simple weather vane, barometer, thermometer, and sundial are included, as well as plans for creating a class weather station. The materials required for the projects are easily accessible, the directions are clear, and the results are bound to produce lots of budding scientists.

Packed with practical hands-on activities and assorted "eye-spy" observations, this book is not intended only to be read—it must be experienced as well. Before engaging your youngsters in the provided activities, give each student a small booklet containing several sheets of blank paper stapled between a construction-paper cover. Have students personalize and label their booklets "My Science Journal." At the conclusion of each science lesson or activity, have students write and date journal entries that describe the day's weather-related discoveries.

What Will The Weather Be?

Written by Lynda DeWitt & Illustrated by Carolyn Croll
Published by Harper Trophy

Part of the notable "Let's-Read-And-Find-Out" science series, this easy reader is packed with primary weather information. Bright drawings illuminate many weather concepts, focusing most clearly on the instruments and the patterns used to predict tomorrow's weather. This book will make a fine introduction to your weather unit.

Cut two large cloud shapes from white paper. Label one cutout "What We Know About Weather Forecasting." Label the remaining cutout "What We Would Like To Know About Weather Forecasting." After reading the book, enlist your students' help in labeling the cutouts with appropriate information. Post both cutouts in your classroom. If possible, arrange in advance for a meteorologist to talk to your students the following day. Students can ask the special guest to provide the answers to their weather-forecasting questions. If a visit from a meteorologist cannot be arranged, help students research the answers to their questions.

It's Raining Cats And Dogs
All Kinds Of Weather, And Why We Have It

Written by Franklyn M. Branley & Illustrated by True Kelley
Published by Houghton Mifflin Company

There's a whirlwind of weather-related tales in this treasure trove of weather history and facts, charts, and projects. Dr. Branley lets kids know which tales are fact and which are truly misconceptions. Lightning never strikes twice? Don't believe that! Can you really do a dance to make it rain? Probably not, but in this book you will find a simple experiment that makes rain in a pan. Discover the different cloud formations and what they mean, and find out about Santa Anas, dancing devils, hurricanes, tornadoes, and more in this irresistible grab bag of weather information.

Whether you use raindrop cutouts or cutouts of cats and dogs, this display is sure to attract lots of interest. Enlist the help of your students in cutting out a supply of desired construction-paper shapes. Attach the title "A Downpour Of Weather Facts" to a bulletin board. At the lower edge of the display mount a colorful umbrella cutout. Each time a new weather fact is introduced, ask one student to write the fact on a cutout and attach the cutout to the display. Splish! Splash! It's raining facts!

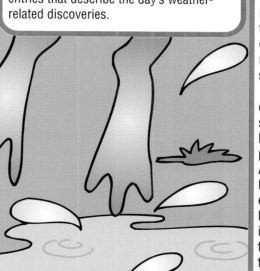

Weather

Written by Seymour Simon
Published by Morrow Junior Books

Noted science writer Seymour Simon lures youngsters on a breathtaking trip through the stratosphere while keeping a sharp eye on the weather. His crystal clear explanations are paired with vivid, panoramic photographs that simplify an understanding of weather conditions and their causes. Clouds, snowflakes, and the etchings of cold winter frost are memorably depicted and should never again go unnoticed by a child who experiences this book.

In the words of the author, "...whatever we decide to do, we can be sure of only two things about the weather: We're going to have it and it's going to change." To practice observing and collecting weather data, give each youngster a copy of the activity on page 98. For each of five days, have the students collect and record data on their weather charts. On the sixth day, divide students into small groups. Ask each group to evaluate the weather information that its members have gathered. Students may then complete the remaining questions independently or collectively within their groups.

Another similarly captivating weather-related book is Seymour Simon's *Storms* (also published by Morrow Junior Books). Using clear concise text and spectacular full-color photographs, the author examines thunderstorms, tornadoes, and hurricanes, and explains how they form and why they die out. Also included are safety guidelines for protecting yourself during these potentially dangerous storms.

Chinook!

Written by Michael O. Tunnell & Illustrated
by Barry Root
Published by Tambourine Books

Most youngsters hear about the devastation of earthquakes, hurricanes, and tornadoes—but a chinook? Use this book to introduce children to a granddaddy blast of warm winter wind that can, in one day, turn a frozen February into a saturated spring with disastrous results. Delightfully illustrated and filled with humor, this story teaches kids about a weird weather phenomenon that won't soon be forgotten.

Author Michael O. Tunnell first encountered the warm winter winds called chinooks while growing up in Alberta, Canada. He readily admits, however, that the chinooks he remembers were not quite like the granddaddy winds described in his story! For a fun writing follow-up, have each youngster write and illustrate a tall tale about a granddaddy chinook. To compile the completed projects into a granddaddy booklet, have each student mount his work on a sizable length of bulletin-board paper. Bind the resulting booklet pages between a slightly larger booklet cover. After each student has presented his page, place the granddaddy booklet in your classroom library for further reading enjoyment.

Hurricane

Written & Illustrated by David Wiesner
Published by Clarion Books

From the deep rich palette of Caldecott-medal winner David Wiesner comes the chronology of a brush with a hurricane as seen through the eyes of two young brothers. What results is a youthful sense of anticipation and adventure for one of nature's most frightening forces—the hurricane.

Well-known for his dreamlike picture books, Wiesner has created another masterpiece to delight children and spark their imaginations. Before reading the book aloud, tell about a favorite tree in your yard or one that you remember from your childhood. Talk about why the tree was special. Ask youngsters to describe favorite trees (or other special locations) around their homes. At the conclusion of the book, discuss the boys' hurricane experience with your students. Emphasize the safety measures that the family took and make a list of weather safety tips that are appropriate for the hazardous weather in your area. For a creative writing follow-up, have each student write and illustrate a story about a weather-related adventure.

The Wind Blew

Written & Illustrated by Pat Hutchins
Published by Aladdin Books

With rhyming verse and colorful illustrations, Pat Hutchins takes the reader on a merry chase after a very capricious wind. Plucking, pulling, whirling, and blowing, the wind gathers a menagerie of items. And just when it appears that the items are lost forever, the wind has a sudden change of heart.

Here's a hands-on activity that creates lots of fun and plenty of wind-related discussion. Take your youngsters outdoors on a breezy day and give each child an empty plastic produce bag. Instruct students to hold their bags open above their heads and turn slowly until the bags fill with air. Have students determine from which direction the wind is blowing and describe the varying strengths of the wind. Ask students to predict what will happen if they let go of their bags, then have them do just that. Repeat this exercise in several locations and compare and contrast the outcomes.

Weather Report

Poems selected by Jane Yolen &
Illustrated by Annie Gusman
Published by
Wordsong • Boyds Mills Press

Acclaimed author Jane Yolen has selected an inspiring collection of weather-related poems for her readers. Sun, rain, snow, wind, and fog are described thoughtfully, playfully, and cleverly by renowned poets including Carl Sandburg, Myra Cohn Livingston, and Robert Frost. This entertaining anthology of poems is perfect for reading aloud to young children.

The poems in this book can be used in a variety of ways throughout your weather unit. In addition to providing plenty of poetry-writing inspiration, students can recite and/or dramatize the poems, copy and illustrate the poems for handwriting practice, and choral-read the poems. Rhyming words and parts of speech can also be explored. The possibilities are endless.

More Books About Weather

The Big Storm
Written & Illustrated by
Bruce Hiscock
Published by Atheneum

Weather Forecasting
Written & Illustrated by
Gail Gibbons
Published by Four Winds Press

It Looked Like Spilt Milk
Written & Illustrated by
Charles G. Shaw
Published by Harper & Row,
Publishers, Inc.

Cloudy With A Chance Of Meatballs
Written by Ron Barrett
Illustrated by Judi Barrett
Published by Aladdin Books

Weather Watching

Use the chart to keep track of the weather for five days.

Day	Degrees	Rain	Wind	Clouds	Sunshine	Other

Answer these questions when your chart is completed.

1. Which day was the warmest? _____

2. Which day was the coolest? _____

3. Did any rain fall? _____ If yes, on which day(s)? _____

    _____

4. How many days were cloudy? _____

5. Which day do you think had the best weather? _____
    Why? _____

6. Why do you think people want to know what the weather will be like? _____

    _____

7. How does the weather affect what you do? _____

    _____

8. What are three jobs that are affected by the weather? _____

    _____

Note To Teacher: Use this activity with *"Weather"* on page 96.

April Showers Bring...Questions!

Rain, lightning, and thunder are weather phenomenons that often pique a child's curiosity. So if it's raining questions in your classroom, provide simple explanations with these hands-on science activities.

ideas by Ann Flagg

Activity 1: Where Do Puddles Go?

You will need:
box of chalk

What to do:
Early in the day, following a rain shower, take the children outdoors to a paved area. Locate a small puddle and draw a chalk outline around it. Ask students to predict what will happen to the puddle as the day continues. Next divide students into small groups and give one person in each group a piece of chalk. Instruct each group to locate a puddle and draw a chalk outline around it. (If desired, have each group mark its outline for easy identification.) Later in the day, after several hours of sunshine, have each group return to its outline and observe how its puddle has changed.

Questions to ask:
1. How did your puddle change?
2. Where do you think the water went?
3. Why do you think some puddles shrank more than others?

This is why:

Water evaporates when water molecules absorb heat. As the sun heats the water in a puddle, the water escapes (or evaporates) into the air in the form of water vapor (an invisible gas). Because heat increases the rate of evaporation, the groups that selected their puddles in sunny locations most likely observed greater evaporation than groups that chose puddles in shady locations.

Activity 2: What Is Rain?

You will need:
one quart-size resealable bag per student
masking tape
permanent marker
warm water tinted with blue food coloring (1/2 cup per student)
measuring cup
funnel
sunny window
student copies of page 101

What to do:
Early in the day, have each student pour one-half cup of blue-tinted, warm water through the funnel and into the bottom of his bag. (The funnel helps keep the sides of the bag dry.) After each student has carefully sealed his bag, use masking tape to attach all the bags to a sunny window as shown. For easy identification, use the marker to label the strips of masking tape with student names. Distribute the activity pages and have the students carefully observe the contents of their bags and complete Observation 1. (Make sure students notice the sides of the bags are dry.)

Later in the day, after the bags have been warmed by the sun, have students examine their bags again and complete Observation 2.

Questions to ask:
1. What do you observe at the top of your bag?
2. Where do you think the droplets of water came from?
3. How are these droplets like raindrops?
4. Does the color of the water droplets surprise you? Why or why not?

Next:
The next day have students repeat the observation process and complete Observation 3.

Questions to ask:
1. How are the water droplets different today? Why?
2. What do you think will happen next?
3. What do you think would happen over the next several days if you slightly opened your bag? Why?

This is why:

Inside the plastic bag is a simple water cycle. As the sun warms the "puddle," the water evaporates and turns to water vapor. Condensation occurs when the water vapor cools. The drops of water on the side of the bag are evidence of this. As drops accumulate on the sides of the bag, they bump against each other and form larger, heavier drops. These heavy drops eventually fall back into the puddle. The water that condenses on the sides of the bag is clear. The food coloring, which is made of solids dissolved in water, stays behind when the water evaporates (much like the dirt in a puddle).

Next:
Have each student complete his activity sheet by labeling the water cycle.

Pam Crane

Activity 3: What Is Lightning?

You will need:
rubber balloon   fluorescent bulb

What to do:
Darken the classroom or take the children into a room with no windows and turn off the lights. (The darker the room, the better the results.) Vigorously rub the balloon on your hair for several seconds; then touch the statically charged balloon to the end of the bulb. This will illuminate the bulb. Turn on the lights and show the youngsters what you did. Repeat the demonstration as many times as desired.

Questions to ask:
1. Why did the bulb light up?
2. What usually makes bulbs light up?
3. How is the spark that lit the bulb like a bolt of lightning?

This is why:

When you rub the balloon on your hair, the balloon builds up an electrical charge (static electricity). Touching the charged balloon to the end of the fluorescent bulb causes the electrical charge to jump from the balloon to the bulb. This illuminates the bulb. Lightning is an electrical discharge within a thunderstorm. As the storm develops, the clouds become charged with electricity. Scientists are still not sure exactly what causes this. But they do know that when the voltage becomes high enough for the electricity to leap across the air from one place to another, lightning flashes. Lightning can spark within a cloud, from one cloud to another, from the ground to a cloud, or from a cloud to the ground.

Activity 4: What Causes Thunder?

You will need:
several paper lunch bags

What to do:
To demonstrate the relationship between thunder and lightning, have one child (Lightning) stand by the classroom light switch(es). Give a second child (Thunder) an opened lunch bag and position him at the front of the classroom facing his classmates. Before beginning the demonstration, explain that thunder is the sound given off by lightning. Then turn off the classroom lights. The demonstration is as follows: Lightning flips the light switch(es) on and off once to represent a bolt of lightning. At the same time, Thunder blows and traps a giant breath of air inside his lunch bag. Then holding the bag securely closed with one hand, he hits the bottom of the air-filled bag with his other hand—BOOM!

This is why:

Thunder is an air explosion—the sound given off by the explosive expansion of air that has been heated by a lightning stroke. When you blow up a paper bag and then bust it, you have created a small explosion of air. Even though thunder and lightning occur simultaneously, the sound of thunder takes much longer to reach us. This is because light travels so much faster than sound. (Light travels at approximately 186,000 **miles** per second. Sound travels at approximately 1,100 **feet** per second.)

Since lightning and thunder occur at the same instant, you can determine the distance to the lightning by measuring the time it takes to hear thunder. As soon as you see lightning, begin counting seconds. (You can count seconds by counting slowly in this way: one thousand one, one thousand two, and so on.) Continue counting until you hear thunder. Then divide the total number of seconds that you counted by five. This number will be how many miles away the lightning struck.

Next:

Repeat the demonstration several times, each time enlisting the help of two different students. For an added challenge, have the remaining students count the seconds (as described above) between the "lightning bolt" and the boom of "thunder." Then as a class determine how far away the "lightning" struck.

Name _____

A Pocketful Of Science:
rain

Learning About Rain

Draw and write what you observe.

Observation 1	**Observation 2**
Date: _____ Time: _____ 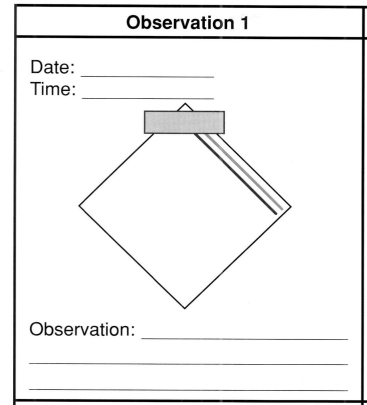 Observation: _____ _____ _____	Date: _____ Time: _____ 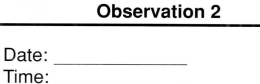 Observation: _____ _____ _____

Observation 3	Compare the water in your bag to the earth's water cycle.
Date: _____ Time: _____ Observation: _____ _____ _____	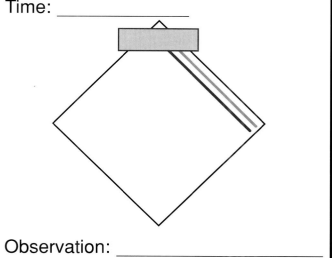 The clouds are like _____ . The rain is like _____ The puddles on the playground are like _____ . a. my blue puddle b. the small droplets at the top of my bag c. the larger drops falling in my bag

©1997 The Education Center, Inc. • *The Best Of* The Mailbox® *Science* • *Primary* • TEC836

Note To Teacher: Use with "Activity 2: What Is Rain?" on page 99.

ON THE MOVE!

AN INTRODUCTION TO THE WATER CYCLE

For a better understanding of nature's water cycle, shower your youngsters with the following activities, experiments, and reproducibles.

ideas by Dr. H. Tu-O

The Wonders Of Water

Make a splash with this brainstorming activity! Divide students into small groups; then challenge the groups to brainstorm ten or more ways that they use water each day. After a predetermined amount of time, ask each group to share its ideas. Compile these ideas on a large raindrop cutout; then display the cutout and the title "The Wonders Of Water." Emphasize that water plays a very important role in everyone's life. In fact without water, no living thing could survive! To entice further interest in water, share these facts:

Facts About Water

- Water covers more than 70 percent of the earth's surface.
- The same water is on earth today that was on earth millions of years ago.
- All living things need water to stay alive.
- All living things contain water. For example, a human body is about 65 percent water, an earthworm is about 80 percent water, and a tomato is about 95 percent water!
- Water is the only substance on earth that is naturally found in three different forms—a liquid, a solid (ice), and a gas (water vapor).
- On average, an American uses about 70 gallons of water a day.

Amazing But True!

Believe it or not, the water on earth today is the same water that was on earth millions of years ago. In fact, you could be drinking water that a dinosaur once stood in or even drank! To help students better understand the natural phenomenon of the water cycle, have them complete the student activity on page 105. Then have students complete the following experiments to demonstrate each water cycle step. If desired, duplicate student copies of the lab sheet on page 106 to use with each of the experiments.

Investigating Evaporation

Evaporation occurs when the heat of the sun causes water to turn into tiny droplets (water vapor) that rise up into the air.

Experiment: A Disappearing Act

To demonstrate evaporation, fill two identical containers about half full of water. Use a crayon or a piece of tape to mark the water level on the outside of each container. Cover one of the containers with foil. Set both containers aside for a few days; then check the water level of each container.

What happens? The water evaporates in both containers. In the uncovered container, the tiny water molecules escape into the air, making the water level go down. In the covered container, the foil stops the water molecules (water vapor) from escaping, so the water level remains high.

Experiment: Heating Up

To demonstrate the effect that heat has on evaporation, fill two identical containers about half full of water. Use a crayon or a piece of tape to mark the water level on the outside of each container. Set one container in a warm place and the other in a cool place. A few days later, check the water level of each container.

What happens? The water stored in the warm place evaporates more quickly than the water stored in the cool place. This happens because when water molecules are warmed, they move faster. The faster water molecules move, the quicker they turn into water vapor and evaporate.

Experiment: Sizing Up Evaporation

To demonstrate different rates of evaporation, fill a wide bowl, a drinking glass, and a narrow jar with the same amount of water. Use a crayon or a piece of tape to mark the water level on the outside of each container. Set the containers aside for a day or two, but do not cover them. A few days later, check the water level of each container.

What happens? The water in the wide bowl evaporates more than the other "bodies of water," because the water in this bowl has a larger surface area. This means there is more space from which the tiny water molecules could escape into the air. The least amount of water evaporates from the narrow jar, because the water in that container has a much smaller surface area.

Contemplating Condensation

Water vapor does not always stay in the air. When water vapor cools, it changes from an invisible gas into tiny droplets of water. This is called *condensation*.

Experiment: Really Cool

To demonstrate condensation, fill two empty drinking glasses: one with warm water and the other one with several ice cubes and cold water. Set the glasses aside for a few minutes.

What happens? The outside of the cold glass becomes wet, but nothing happens to the outside of the warm glass. When the water vapor in the air touches the cold glass, it is cooled. This causes the vapor to turn into tiny water droplets. When the water vapor in the air touches the warm glass, it is not cooled and does not condense.

Experiment: Hot Air

Another way to demonstrate condensation is to place a mirror a few inches away from your mouth, then exhale onto the mirror.

What happens? The air is filled with water vapor. When air is inhaled, it is warmed by the body. When the air is exhaled, it touches cool air. This causes the water vapor to cool off and turn into tiny water droplets. The condensation can be seen on the mirror. This same experiment can be done on a cold day by just exhaling into the cold air.

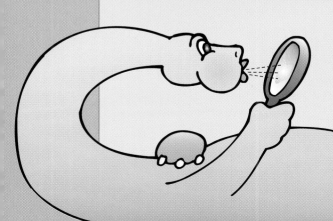

103

Pondering Precipitation

When water vapor condenses, it turns into tiny water droplets that form clouds. As each droplet falls through the cloud, it combines with other droplets. This results in *precipitation*. Precipitation is any moisture that falls from clouds—rain, snow, hail, or sleet.

Experiment: Making Rain (to be demonstrated by an adult)

To demonstrate precipitation, boil water in a teakettle. Wait until steam begins to escape from the teakettle. Then, wearing oven mitts, hold a tray of ice cubes about five inches above the steam.

What happens? The water from the kettle evaporates (steam). The tiny droplets of water collect where the air is cool (ice cube tray). When several water droplets combine beneath the tray, a raindrop is formed and it falls downward.

Completing The Cycle

To demonstrate the complete water cycle, have each of several small groups of students make a terrarium. By observing this simplified version of the water cycle for the next few weeks, students will observe *evaporation* (water evaporates from the soil, the pond, and the plants), *condensation* (water droplets form on the lid), and *precipitation* (drops of water fall down into the soil). For a culminating activity, have each student illustrate and label this water cycle on a large sheet of drawing paper.

Materials needed for one terrarium:
a large glass jar with a screw-on lid
small stones to cover the bottom of the jar
potting soil
several small plants or root cuttings from houseplants (If root cuttings are used, place them in water several days before the activity to promote root growth.)
a small jar lid
water

What to do:
Cover the bottom of the clean dry jar with stones; then add about a four-inch layer of potting soil. Position each small plant in the soil as desired, making sure that all roots are covered. Water the plants until the soil is moist. Fill a small jar lid with water and set it among the plants to create a pond. Screw the lid tightly on the jar. Place the jar in a well-lighted area, but out of direct sunlight.

Reading About The Water Cycle

Here are two books about the water cycle that you won't want to miss. Ask your media specialist for assistance in locating other appropriate titles.

The Magic School Bus At The Waterworks by Joanna Cole (Scholastic Inc., 1986). Who would have thought that learning about water could be so much fun? In this delightful book, Ms. Frizzle and her students take an unforgettable field trip to the waterworks.

The Water's Journey by Eleonore Schmid (North-South Books, 1989). Beginning with a freshly fallen blanket of snow, this beautifully illustrated book takes the reader through the water's cycle.

The Water Cycle

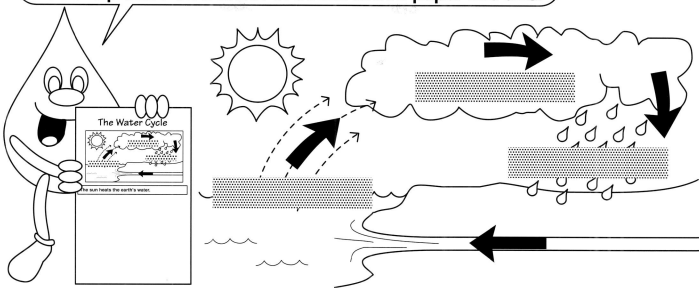

Color the picture. Then cut it out.
Glue the picture on a sheet of construction paper like this.

The Water Cycle

The sun heats the earth's water.

Cut out the sentence strips.
Glue the strips below the picture in the right order.

The water droplets become heavy.

As the water vapor rises, it cools down.

The sun heats the earth's water.

The heavy droplets fall to the earth as rain, snow, sleet, or hail.

The warmed water turns into vapor and rises in the air.

In the clouds the tiny water droplets join together.

The tiny water droplets form clouds.

The cooled water vapor forms tiny droplets of water.

Cut out the words.
Glue each word in the correct box on the picture.

precipitation   condensation   evaporation

Note To Teacher: Use with "Amazing But True!" on page 102. Each student needs a 9" x 12" sheet of construction paper to complete this activity.

Lab Sheet

Name _____

Experiment _____

This is what I did: _____

_____

_____

_____

This is what happened: _____

_____

_____

_____

Just dropping by to say...

earned this shower of praise for

Note To Teacher: To use the lab sheet, see "Amazing But True!" on page 102. Duplicate and present the awards to students as desired.

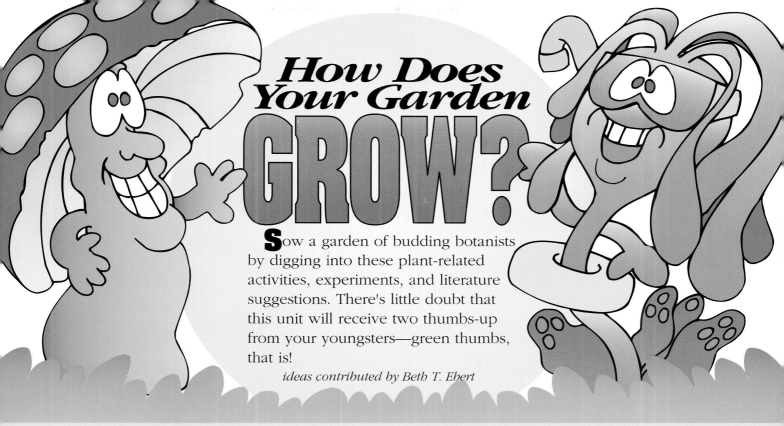

How Does Your Garden GROW?

Sow a garden of budding botanists by digging into these plant-related activities, experiments, and literature suggestions. There's little doubt that this unit will receive two thumbs-up from your youngsters—green thumbs, that is!

ideas contributed by Beth T. Ebert

Write On!

Individual journals are just what budding botanists need to record daily observations, plant facts, breakthrough discoveries, and more! To make a journal, use the patterns on page 110 to duplicate a construction-paper cover and a supply of blank journal pages. Staple the pages between the duplicated cover and a piece of equal-sized construction paper (back cover). Have students personalize their journals as desired, then keep them handy for recording plant-worthy data. See the ideas that follow for more journal-writing suggestions.

To Bloom Or Not To Bloom

Introduce youngsters to the wonderful world of plants with two outstanding books written by Ruth Heller. *The Reason For A Flower* and *Plants That Never Ever Bloom* are both bursting with information about the plant world. After reading each book, have students recall what they learned as you list their responses on a large cutout related to the book (such as a flower or a mushroom). Post the cutout and continue to add information to it throughout your plant study. If desired, encourage students to write the facts that they found most interesting about blooming and nonblooming plants in their journals.

Stepping Into Seed Collection

As students learned in Ruth Heller's book *The Reason For A Flower,* seeds travel in a variety of fashions. For a fun activity, ask youngsters to bring in adult socks that can be slipped over their shoes. (Wool socks work best for this activity, but any socks are fine.) When you have a pair of socks per student, you are ready to step into seed collecting! Before leaving the room, have each youngster slip a sock over each of her shoes. Then take your students for a walk through a field or other weedy area. Seeds, burs, stickers, and weeds of all kinds will stick to the socks. Back in the classroom, have students carefully remove the items that they carried inside on their socks. If desired, have students place their collections in paper baking cups.

After discussing the types of things that were collected, ask students to brainstorm where the seeds in their collections might have originally come from. Then have each youngster glue or tape one seed from her collection onto a sheet of paper (or a journal page), and write and illustrate a story as if she were the seed. Encourage youngsters to write about where their journeys began, the sights they have seen along the way, and how they think their journeys will end. Then invite your budding authors to share their creations!

Taking A Closer Look

This science center takes only a minute to set up and it provides hours of enjoyable learning opportunities. In a safe location, display a microscope and a variety of seeds. If you have completed a seed-collecting activity such as "Stepping Into Seed Collection," simply have students place the extra seeds from their collections at the center. (For easy storage, place seeds in empty egg cartons, storing all like seeds in the same egg cup.) Otherwise, challenge youngsters to bring in an assortment of seeds (in egg cartons) to be placed at the center. Each student can take a microscopic look at the outside and inside of several seeds. Wow! Look what's inside!

A Plant-Tasting Affair

After familiarizing students with the parts of a plant, they'll be ready to organize a plant snack! To begin, have students brainstorm foods they eat that are plants. Write their responses on the chalkboard. Then, using colored chalk, circle the listed items to show the different plant parts. For example, draw green circles around plant leaves (such as cabbage, lettuce, and spinach), yellow circles around fruits and seeds (such as tomatoes, corn, oats, sunflowers, bananas, and coconut), pink circles around stems (such as celery, asparagus, and chives), and brown circles around roots (such as carrots, onions, potatoes, and beets). On the day of the snack, ask each student to bring a food sample (for three people) of each plant part. Arrange the snacks by plant parts on a long table. Then let the snacking begin. Encourage each youngster to sample at least one food from each category. If desired, have students note the foods that they ate in their journals.

Green Thumbs, Unite

This hands-on approach to scientific exploration may be dirty work, but it's educationally enlightening. You will need one clear plastic cup and one self-sticking label per child, a variety of planting mediums (such as potting soil, red or black clay, peat moss, and sand), and a supply of seeds. You may also wish to enlist the help of three adult volunteers. Divide students into three groups and assign each group one of the following cases:

Depth Finders—The students in this group experiment to determine how the depth at which seeds are planted affects their growth. Each student plants four seeds, each at a different depth, in a cup of potting soil. Next the student personalizes his self-sticking label and notes the depth of each seed. Then he attaches the label to his cup.

Soil Sleuths—The students in this group experiment to determine which planting medium best promotes plant growth. Working as a group to avoid duplications, each student fills his cup with a different plant medium or combination of plant mediums. Next he notes on his personalized label what plant medium(s) he used. After students have attached their labels, have each student plant four seeds in his cup. All students should use the same procedure to plant their seeds.

Population Controllers—The students in this group experiment to determine the effects of overcrowding on plant growth. Each student fills his cup with potting soil. Then, beginning with four seeds and increasing one seed per child, each youngster plants a different number of seeds in his cup. All students should use the same procedure to plant their seeds.

When the planting is completed, have each student water his project; then set up a watering schedule for all students to follow. Instruct each youngster to observe his project daily, then write about his observation in his journal. When appropriate, have each group meet to determine and announce its findings.

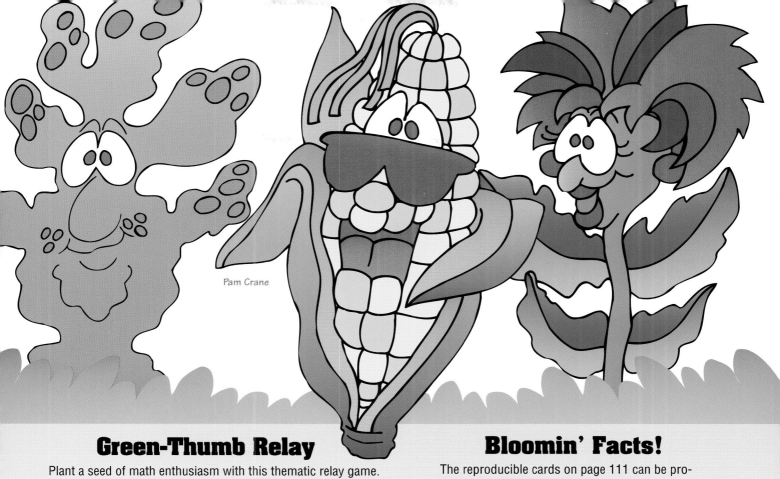

Pam Crane

Green-Thumb Relay

Plant a seed of math enthusiasm with this thematic relay game. Before introducing the game, have students glue 30 laminated, bloom-shaped calendar cutouts to Popsicle-stick stems. Code half of the stems to represent one set of game pieces. Leave the other set of 15 stems uncoded. Using a permanent marker, program one set of blooms with math problems; then program the other set to match. Each set should contain five problems that are equal to each of three solutions. Then label three plastic pots with these solutions for each set of cutouts.

To play, divide students into two teams. Opposite each team place a set of three pots and a set of flowers (facedown) atop a table. In relay fashion, competing team members approach the table, pick the first available flower, and plant it in the appropriate pot. Play continues in this manner. If a player notices that a teammate incorrectly planted a flower, he may use his turn to replant it. When all flowers are planted, award two points for each correctly placed flower. The team with the most points wins!

"Be-Leaf" It Or Not!

Discover for yourself that a plant can stimulate your students' reading desires! Place a fast-growing ivy or sweet potato plant in your independent reading area. Inform students that some gardeners believe that talking to plants helps them grow faster. Explain that you believe, based on this assumption, that reading to a plant should make the plant flourish! Measure the plant; then encourage students to read orally to the plant each day. Each week, as a class activity, measure and calculate the plant's growth. Your youngsters' oral reading skills are sure to blossom!

Bloomin' Facts!

The reproducible cards on page 111 can be programmed for Plant Concentration. To make a set of Concentration cards, a student needs two copies of page 111. He programs the cards on one page with plant-related questions and the cards on the remaining page with corresponding answers. Then the student mounts both pages onto construction paper and cuts out the individual cards. The cards can also be programmed as vocabulary cards, flash cards, or task cards. There are "planty" of possibilities!

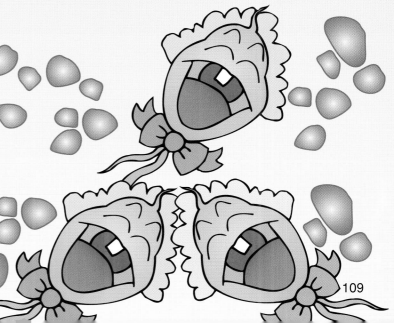

_____'s
PLANT
Journal

Note To Teacher: Use with "Write On!" on page 107.

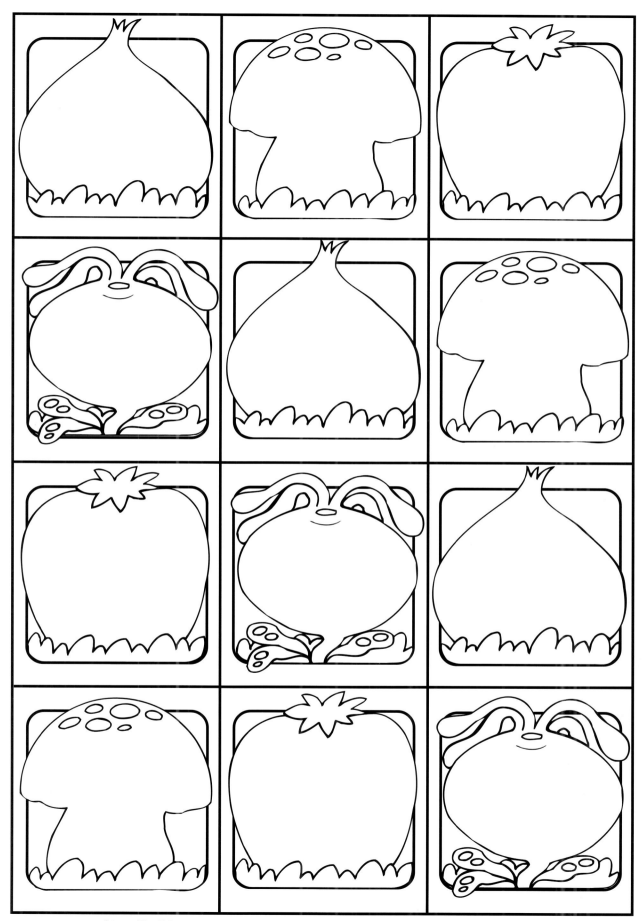

Note To Teacher: Use with "Bloomin' Facts!" on page 109.

This Place Is Dry!

Exploring The Desert

The desert is definitely dry, but that doesn't mean it's a dry topic of study! Use this collection of activities and reproducibles to investigate an intriguing ecosystem that's home to some unique plants and animals. You're sure to have a hot time!

What Is A Desert?

Most scientists agree that for an environment to be a true desert, it must receive less than ten inches of precipitation per year and have a high rate of evaporation. The following ditty is a fun way to acquaint your youngsters with the desert environment. Post the lyrics; then adapt them to the tune of "Oh! Susanna." Invite students to create additional verses as they learn more about the desert.

Welcome To The Desert

Oh, the days are hot; the nights are cold;
The weather it is dry.
With rocks and sand and lots of space.
Sometimes the wind blows by.

Chorus:
Come see the desert—it's a pretty place to be!
Just keep your cool and watch your step,
For you may have company!

Look, there's a giant cactus tree.
Saguaro is its name.
It stores water for dry times,
And you should do the same.

Chorus

When the sun goes down, the air turns cool.
More critters start to roam.
They're hungry and they search for food.
The desert is their home.

Chorus

The centipedes and scorpions
Are poisonous as can be.
So keep your distance—don't you touch!
There's plenty more to see!

Meet The Desert!

Not all deserts are hot.

No two deserts are exactly the same.

Many desert animals hide during the day.

Some desert animals do not drink.

Birds nest in a saguaro cactus.

A Bloomin' Cactus!

It only takes a minute to turn tissue-paper squares into colorful cactus blossoms. To make one blossom, stack four 6-inch squares of tissue paper. Fold the stacked squares in half and in half again; then staple the folded corner. Trim to round each unstapled corner. Gently pull the tissue paper apart to open the blossom. Use the colorful blooms to decorate the research project described in "A Prickly Approach," the cactus folder described in "A Barrel Of Vocabulary" on page 113, and other cactus-related projects.

A Prickly Approach

Take this prickly approach to desert research and earn rave reviews! You will need one large cactus-pad cutout labeled "Meet The Desert" and a supply of small cactus pads—all cut from green paper.

Mount the labeled pad at the lower edge of a large display area. Each time a new desert fact is discovered, a student writes the fact on a cactus pad cutout and attaches the programmed pad to the display. In no time your prickly pear cactus will be growing by leaps and bounds. At the conclusion of your unit, have each youngster craft a cactus blossom and attach it to the display. (See "A Bloomin' Cactus!") Toothpick spines can also be added. Keep this striking project on display as a reminder of your desert studies.

Michele Converse Baerns—Gr. 2, Sevierville Primary School, Sevierville, TN

A Barrel Of Vocabulary

Create a thirst for desert-related vocabulary with cactus-shaped vocabulary folders. To make a folder like the one shown, begin with a 12" x 18" sheet of green construction paper. Fold and crease the paper to create a pocket; then trim the folded paper into the shape of a barrel cactus. (If desired, provide a tagboard template for students to trace.) Glue the outer edges of the pocket together. Personalize the pocket; then glue a tissue-paper blossom (see "A Bloomin' Cactus!" on page 112) and toothpick spines to the project.

Securely staple the completed folders to a bulletin board and provide a supply of blank construction-paper strips. Each morning post a different vocabulary word at the display. A student copies the word onto a blank strip, researches the meaning of the word, and writes and/or illustrates its meaning on the blank side of her word strip. She then stores her completed vocabulary project in her cactus folder. Your youngsters' desert vocabularies are sure to blossom!

Where Are The Deserts?

Deserts cover about one-fifth of the world's land, but where are they? Using the reproducible map on page 116, take students on a desert discovery mission. Introduce the map key and color code. Review what makes an environment a desert, and have students ponder the meaning of *semidesert.* Then help students conclude that a semidesert region is very much like a desert except that it receives a little more rainfall. This additional precipitation means a greater number of plants and animals can grow and survive there.

To complete the mapping activity, lead students from continent to continent. As students color their maps, share related facts from "Did You Know?" Point out that the Arctic region and the continent of Antarctica are not shown on the map. Explain that some scientists call these areas deserts because they have less than ten inches of rainfall a year. However, other scientists disagree, arguing that a true desert must also have a high rate of evaporation—something that these two areas do not. When the maps have been completed, challenge students to find out on which deserts the pictured wildlife can be found (see page 160 for locations).

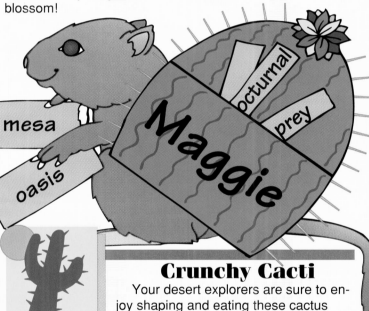

Did You Know?

Share these facts with your students as they complete the mapping activity described in "Where Are The Deserts?"

- The Sahara Desert in northern Africa is about the size of the United States. It is the largest desert in the world.
- The Gobi Desert in eastern Asia is the coldest desert in the world.
- Almost half of Australia is covered by desert.
- The sandiest desert in the world is the Arabian Desert.
- The Atacama Desert in South America is the driest desert in the world—some of its areas haven't had any rainfall for over 13 years!
- South America's Patagonian Desert is one of the least studied deserts because it is very difficult to reach.
- North American deserts are home to many plants, animals, and people. An air force base is located in the Mohave Desert!

Crunchy Cacti

Your desert explorers are sure to enjoy shaping and eating these cactus look-alikes. This recipe makes approximately 15 to 20 crunchy cacti.

Ingredients:
1 12-oz. package butterscotch chips
2 tablespoons peanut butter   1 6-oz. can chow mein noodles
green food coloring   waxed paper

Directions:
1. Melt chips over low heat, stirring occasionally.
2. Stir in peanut butter and desired amount of green food coloring.
3. Add chow mein noodles and stir until well coated.
4. Remove from heat. Allow the mixture to cool until it is safe to handle.
5. Working atop waxed paper, have each child fashion a golf-ball-size portion of the mixture into a cactus shape.
6. When the projects have hardened, have each student peel his cactus from the paper and chow down!

Michele Converse Baerns—Gr. 2, Sevierville Primary School Sevierville, TN

Cactus Country

Cacti are the most well-known desert plants, but other plants grow in deserts too. All desert plants have one thing in common—a method of gathering and storing water so that they can survive without regular rainfall.

A cactus uses its roots to gather and store water. Show students a picture of a barrel cactus and explain that this cactus also stores water in its stem. To show how this happens, have students stand side by side in a circle formation and imagine that they are part of a large barrel cactus. Ask the students to use their voices to create the sounds of rain; then instruct them to make slurping sounds as if the cactus is soaking up water through its roots. Next have the students join hands, then slowly and carefully step backward until their arms are extended. Ask the students to describe how this demonstration compares to a barrel cactus storing water; then have the students act out what will happen to the cactus after several weeks of hot, dry weather.

Amazing Animals

The bodies of many desert animals are designed for life on the desert. The camel is a perfect example. Bushy eyebrows and long eyelashes protect a camel's eyes from the sand and sun. Its nostrils close between breaths so that sand does not enter its nose. A camel's broad feet keep it from sinking in the sand. And what about that hump? Well, it doesn't contain water as it was once believed. Instead it stores fat that breaks down into food when no food is available to eat. Students will enjoy investigating desert animals to discover how their bodies help them cope with desert life. Record students' findings on a chart like the one shown. Then, using the knowledge they have gained, have each student illustrate a make-believe desert animal and in a written paragraph explain how this animal copes with life in the desert. Be sure to set aside time for students to share their unique creations with their classmates!

Denise Donahue, Berlin, MD

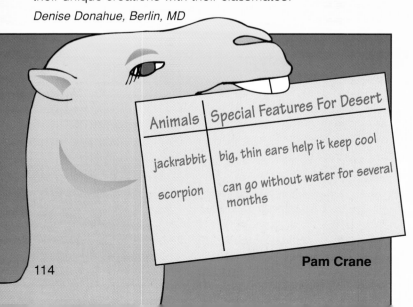

Animals	Special Features For Desert
jackrabbit	big, thin ears help it keep cool
scorpion	can go without water for several months

Pam Crane

Beating The Heat

Desert animals have different ways of coping with the extreme desert heat. Some animals can tolerate high desert temperatures and seek shade only during the hottest part of the day. Other animals escape the heat by hiding in burrows, dens, or protected shelters. As the sun sets and the desert begins to cool, these animals come out of hiding and begin their search for food. Use the project on page 117 to introduce students to three *diurnal* (daytime) and three *nocturnal* (nighttime) desert animals.

Duplicate page 117 on white construction paper and have each youngster color a copy. To complete his project, a student cuts out patterns A and B on the bold lines. Then he cuts along the dotted lines to create one large window and three small ones in cutout A. (Provide assistance as needed.) Next the student stacks cutout A atop cutout B, aligns the edges, and pokes a brad through the black dots, joining both cutouts. To view diurnal animals, the student positions the daytime sky in the large window. When the nighttime sky is featured, nocturnal animals are on display.

A Colossal Cactus

The saguaro cactus—which can grow to be 50 feet tall—is very impressive! The more water it stores, the heavier it becomes. In fact a saguaro cactus can weigh as much as an elephant! The cactus is covered with very sharp spines, and if the plant has "arms," it must be at least 50 years old. During its life span of approximately 200 years, the cactus is alive with activity, providing food and shelter for a variety of desert wildlife. *Desert Giant* by Barbara Bash provides an in-depth look at this colossal cactus.

For a fun follow-up project, have each student design a desert scene featuring a saguaro cactus. First have each child trace his hand and forearm on a 9" x 12" sheet of green construction paper to create a shape similar to the one shown. A student cuts on the outline and mounts the resulting saguaro shape on a 12" x 18" sheet of construction paper. He then uses construction-paper scraps, toothpicks, and crayons or markers to create his desert scene.

Karen Faas Marovich, Erie, PA

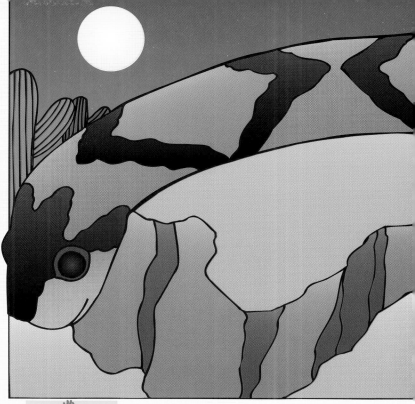

A Walk In The Desert

This booklet-making project takes students on a stroll through the desert! Each youngster needs a tan construction-paper copy of the desert tortoise pattern on page 118, and white construction-paper copies of pages 119 and 120. Distribute pages 119 and 120. After each student has personalized and decorated his booklet cover, read and discuss the information presented on each booklet page before students complete their independent work. Then have each child cut out his booklet cover and pages on the dotted lines and stack them in sequential order. Distribute page 118, and instruct each student to color and cut out the desert tortoise pattern. Then help each youngster staple his booklet project to the cutout as indicated.

Karen Faas Marovich, Erie, PA

A One-Of-A-Kind Dessert

Looking for a tasteful way to wrap up your desert studies? Try this cake-decorating idea! You will need a large, frosted yellow sheet cake and a variety of decorating supplies like crushed vanilla wafers for sand, whole vanilla wafers for desert landforms, a batch of blue Jell-O® Jigglers™ for an oasis, popped popcorn or caramel corn for tumbleweeds, small sweet pickles for cacti, stick pretzels and green icing for palm trees, gummy candies (snakes, lizards, spiders, etc.), and animal crackers (camels, coyotes, rabbits, etc.). Be creative!

As a class, design a desired desert scene on the chalkboard. Then, after everyone has washed and dried his hands, have each student in turn contribute to decorating the frosted cake—creating the desert scene designed by the class. Now that's a dandy desert dessert!

Karen Walden—Gr. 1, Ravenel Elementary, Seneca, SC

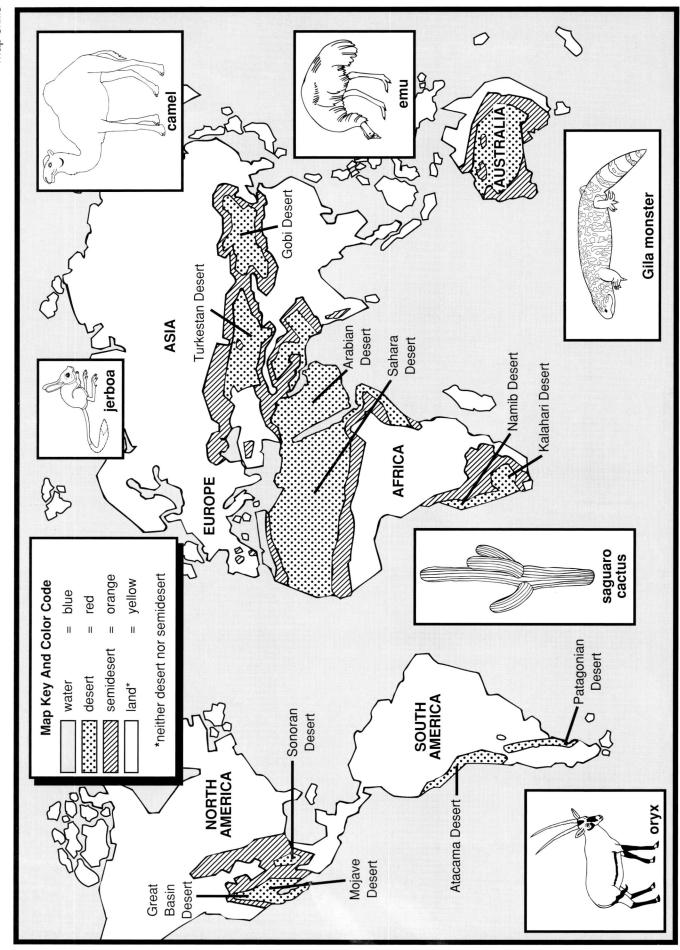

Map Key And Color Code

water	=	blue
desert	=	red
semidesert	=	orange
land*	=	yellow

*neither desert nor semidesert

camel

emu

jerboa

AUSTRALIA

Gila monster

saguaro cactus

oryx

Gobi Desert
Turkestan Desert
ASIA
EUROPE
Arabian Desert
Sahara Desert
AFRICA
Namib Desert
Kalahari Desert

NORTH AMERICA
Great Basin Desert
Sonoran Desert
Mojave Desert

SOUTH AMERICA
Atacama Desert
Patagonian Desert

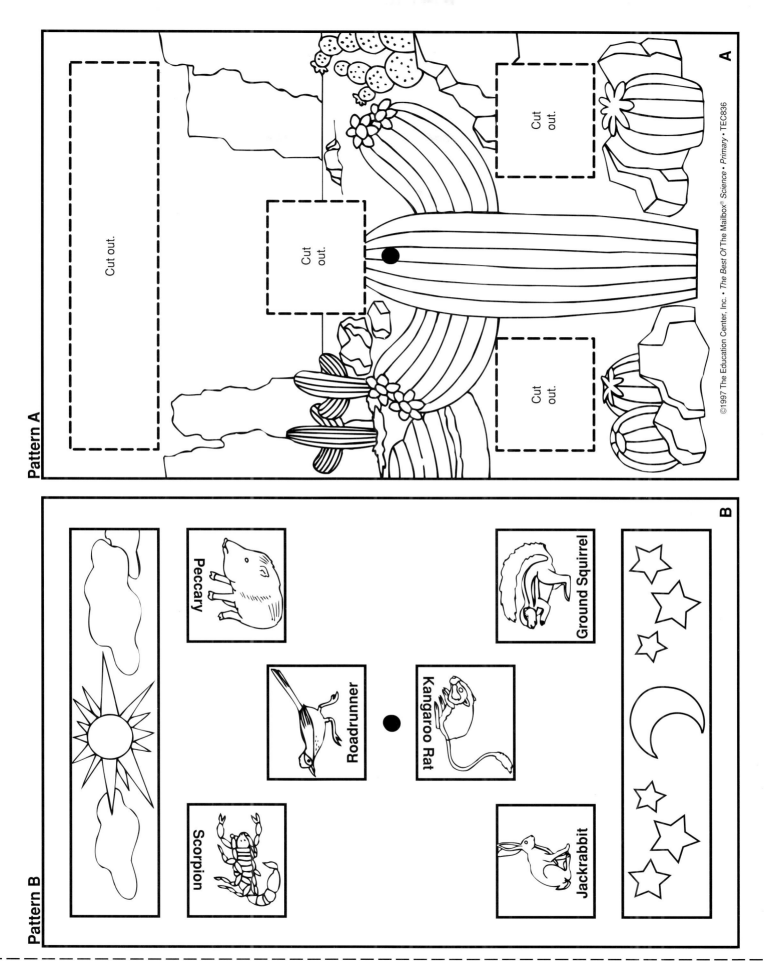

Pattern A

A

Cut out.

Cut out.

Cut out.

Cut out.

©1997 The Education Center, Inc. • *The Best Of The Mailbox® Science • Primary •* TEC836

Pattern B

B

Peccary

Ground Squirrel

Roadrunner

Kangaroo Rat

Scorpion

Jackrabbit

Note To Teacher: Use with "Beating The Heat" on page 114.

117

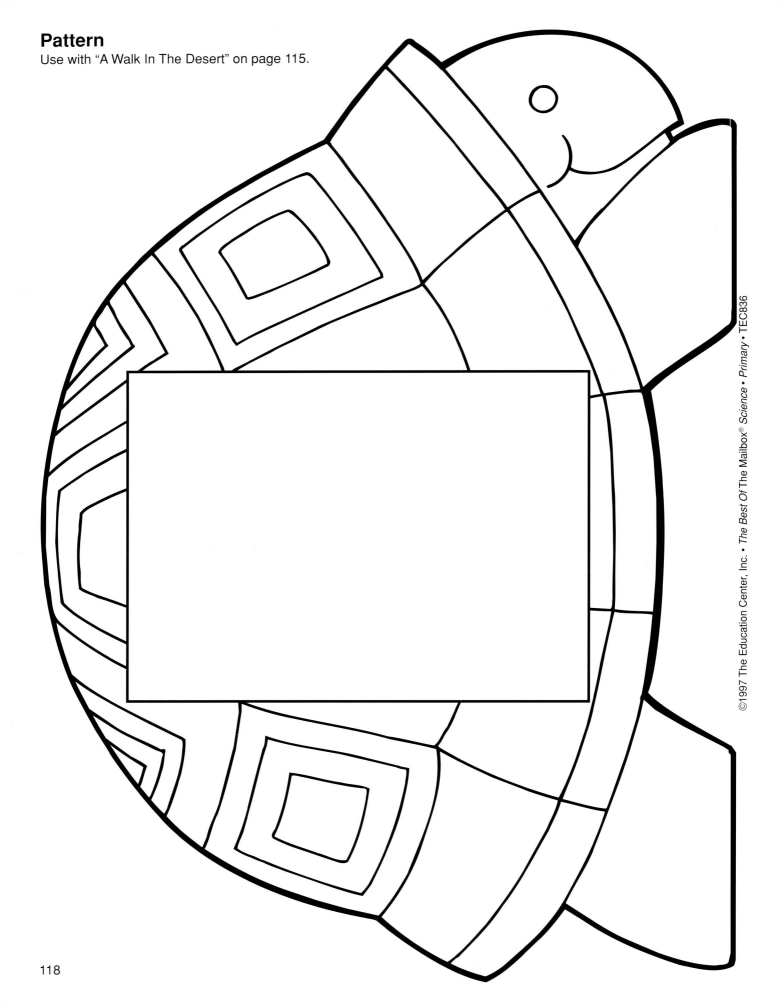

A
Walk In The
Desert

by

_____

A desert is a very dry place. This is a picture of a desert.

1

A desert has many kinds of plants. This is a picture of my favorite desert plant.

It is a _____.

2

A desert has many kinds of animals. This is a picture of my favorite desert animal.

It is a _____.

3

Note To Teacher: Use with "A Walk In The Desert" on page 115.

119

This is a picture of an animal that hunts during the day.

It is a _____ .

4

This is a picture of an animal that hunts at night.

It is a _____ .

5

Deserts can be very different. This is me on a desert in

_____ .

6

I think the desert is an interesting place because _____

_____

_____

_____

_____

_____

_____

_____

_____

_____

_____ .

7

Note To Teacher: Use with "A Walk In The Desert" on page 115.

A Literary Oasis

The deserts of the world may be dry, but this expansive selection of desert-related literature certainly isn't! Use these hot books to introduce and enhance your study of an extraordinary ecosystem.

books reviewed by Deborah Zink Roffino

Fun-To-Read Fiction

Alejandro's Gift

Written by Richard E. Albert & Illustrated by Sylvia Long
Chronicle Books, 1994
The furrows in Alejandro's ancient brow match the primal creases in the dry, desert earth. Alejandro lives alone in a small adobe house on a lonely desert road. His burro is his only companion. To pass the lonely hours, Alejandro plants a garden that—much to his surprise—cultivates a powerful lesson about nature and friendship. This beautifully illustrated story will prompt children to look at the world around them in a new way. An illustrated glossary, featuring some of the desert wildlife presented, adds to the appeal of this already superb book.

The Three Little Javelinas

Written by Susan Lowell & Illustrated by Jim Harris
Northland Publishing Company, 1992
This chili-flavored adaptation of *The Three Little Pigs* is definitely hot! Scurrying from a tumbleweed shack to a saguaro-rib hut to an adobe-brick house, three little *javelinas* (wild pigs of the Sonoran Desert) try to outwit a huffing, puffing, big, bad coyote. Dressed in cowboy duds and prepared for life in the rugged desert, these three little piglets are more than this coyote bargained for!

Notable Nonfiction

Here Is The Southwestern Desert

Written by Madeleine Dunphy & Illustrated by Anne Coe
Hyperion Books For Children, 1995
Here is a read-aloud masterpiece with gallery-caliber artwork! The story reveals the elements that build the chain of life in the Sonoran Desert. Cumulative text threads alongside breathtaking landscapes in energetic hues. The result is an unforgettable, factual tale that is a visual and linguistic treat!

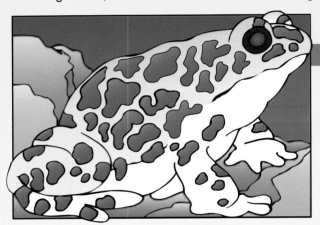

Look Closer: Desert Life

Written by Barbara Taylor & Photographed by Frank Greenaway
Dorling Kindersley, Inc.; 1992
There are plenty of strange-looking critters roaming the deserts of the world, and this striking examination brings youngsters nose to nose with some of the most outrageous. Splendid photos overwhelm the pages, capturing the slimy, spindly, craggy, gnarly hides that are detailed in the primary text. Sure to get a reaction from young readers, this volume is memorable, informative, and highly entertaining.

Desert Giant: The World Of The Saguaro Cactus

Written & Illustrated by Barbara Bash
Little, Brown And Company; 1989
Intense colors brighten the pages of this fascinating Reading Rainbow® book. The giant saguaro cactus—stalwart symbol of the Sonoran Desert— is superbly introduced as the cactus that can grow as tall as 50 feet, weigh up to several tons, and live for 200 years! Readers learn that appearing barren and forlorn is only this cactus's public persona. In truth this colossal cactus is alive with activity! Youngsters will, without a doubt, come away with a better understanding of—and a lasting respect for—this desert giant.

Vanishing Cultures: Sahara

Written & Photographed by Jan Reynolds
Harcourt Brace & Company, 1991
Author and photographer Jan Reynolds traveled to the largest desert on Earth to capture on film the Tuareg's unique way of desert life. A nomadic people, the Tuareg have lived in the heart of the Sahara for centuries. Now— because of outside influences—their ancient way of life is rapidly disappearing. Reynold's dramatic photographs and simple text beckon readers to experience the vanishing culture of a fascinating desert people.

Where The Buffalo Roam

Adapted & Illustrated by Jacqueline Geis
Ideals Children's Books, 1992
Youngsters explore the diverse life and landforms of the Southwest through an expanded verse of the well-known song "Home On The Range." Soft watercolor paintings feature the varied faces of the American Southwest from the wide, grassy plains; through the harsh-yet-lovely desert; to the Rocky Mountain foothills. An abundance of protected, threatened, and endangered species are featured.

One Small Square: Cactus Desert

Written by Donald M. Silver & Illustrated by Patricia J. Wynne
W. H. Freeman And Company, 1995

Part of a phenomenal science series that investigates small squares of our Earth, this reference book is an excellent choice for your desert unit. Cutaways, close-ups, and panoramic vistas show off the details of the desert. The text and sketches overflow with data, while the sidebars suggest experiments. It's the ultimate desert field trip. Young desert researchers will appreciate the desert life classifications and comprehensive index located at the back of the book.

Watching Desert Wildlife

Written by Caroline Arnold & Photographed by Arthur Arnold
Carolrhoda Books, Inc.; 1994

A brief introduction to the deserts of the world is followed up by a journey of discovery that takes readers through the deserts of North America. Stunning photographs uncover a variety of desert wildlife. The somewhat lengthy text reveals some of the techniques that these plants and animals employ for survival in their harsh and arid environments. An excellent reference for research projects.

Pam Crane

The Desert Alphabet Book

Written by Jerry Pallotta & Illustrated by Mark Astrella
Charlesbridge Publishing, 1994

Life on the desert unfolds between the covers of this vibrant book. From *A* to *Z,* a kid-pleasing assortment of desert wildlife and terms are explored. The traces of humor that are woven into the easy-to-read text reflect the author's understanding of the audience for whom he writes. A perfect learning tool for youngsters studying arid lands.

Discover My World: Desert

Written by Ron Hirschi & Illustrated by Barbara Bash
Bantam Books, 1992

Explore the mysterious desert world and meet some of the animals that live there. The lyrical text of renowned environmentalist Ron Hirschi invites youngsters to guess the identity of the desert dweller that is being presented on each colorful spread. A boxed clue provides visual assistance. Additional information about the discovered desert dwellers can be found at the back of the book.

Imagine Living Here: This Place Is Dry

Written by Vicki Cobb & Illustrated by Barbara Lavallee
Walker And Company, 1989

What might it be like to live on the Sonoran Desert in Arizona? This colorful paperback is packed with information describing the living conditions of this dry place. Meet Americans who live among the snakes, spiders, roadrunners, and cacti of this southwestern desert. Imagine that!

A Treasure Chest Of Life

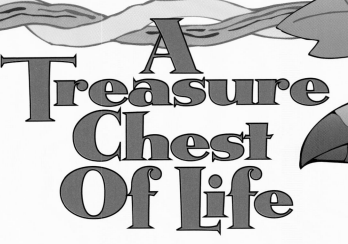

The Tropical Rain Forest

Tropical rain forests overflow with their own kinds of precious gems—unique plants and animals. But, like most treasure, it will quickly vanish if handled recklessly. Venture into the rain forest with the following thematic activities and reproducibles. It's the perfect opportunity to promote an appreciation for an irreplaceable fortune and to plant seeds of thought for preservation.

ideas by Theresa Ives Audet, Karen Gibson, and Ann Flagg

A One-Of-A-Kind Journey

Peer into the thick, leafy canopy of a tropical rain forest and what will you see? Over half of the world's species of plants and animals. Oxygen suppliers and a crucial link in the water cycle. Tribal groups who live in much the same way as their Stone Age ancestors. Huge trees holding soil in place, preventing floods and erosion. Rare plants that provide vital ingredients for medicines. A vast array of irreplaceable riches—that's what you'll see.

But the tropical rain forest is fast becoming a vanishing area. At a rate of 100 acres per minute, rain forests are being cut down to make room for cash crops, dams, farms, cattle ranches, and logging operations. Because of recent conservation efforts, your students may already know a thing or two about the rain forest. Start your journey into the rain forest by finding out what your students already know. List their ideas on a large poster, perhaps cut into the shape of a treasure chest. Post the resulting list and continue to add facts to it throughout your rain forest exploration.

From Top To Bottom

The rain forest, with its millions of plants and animals, forms a special community or *ecosystem*. From the top of the trees to beneath the forest floor, all parts of the community work together to make sure that the rain forest thrives. Use the following information to introduce the layers of life found in a rain forest.

Emergent Layer: The tallest trees scattered throughout the rain forest are called *emergents*. There are usually only one or two of these towering trees (115 to 250 feet tall) per acre. Most emergents have small leaves and slender trunks. Birds such as the toucan and the macaw find refuge and a bird's-eye view of the forest in these treetops.

Canopy: The canopy has trees 65–100 feet in height. These trees, along with the emergents, form a covering over the forest that acts like a giant umbrella or canopy. Here sunlight and rain are plentiful. The woody vines, called *lianas,* that twist around the trunks of rain forest trees sprout leaves in the welcomed light. Since many varieties of nuts and fruits grow in the canopy layer, the animals that feast on them make their homes here too. The slow-moving sloth is one famous canopy dweller. The lovely vanilla orchid, from which vanilla is extracted, blooms in the canopy.

Understory: Small trees that rarely grow beyond 15 feet in height, and a shorter layer of very young canopy trees, shrubs, ferns, and palms, can be found in the understory. Beneath them are still smaller bushes, ferns, and woody vines. Because of the lack of sunlight, few flowers bloom in this layer. The layer is often hot and humid because the heat and moisture of the forest are trapped beneath the canopy. Spider monkeys swing from the vines, and the blue morpha butterfly flits and flutters in the understory.

Forest Floor: Although mosses, herbs, fungi, seedlings, ferns, and bromeliads grow on the forest floor, the vegetation is sparse—mainly because of the lack of sunlight. High temperatures and humidity make decomposition exceedingly rapid. Anteaters, scorpions, and a variety of insects roam the forest floor.

Water, Water Everywhere

The term *rain forest* was first coined by a German botanist in 1898. He used the term to describe forests that grow in constantly wet conditions. In most rain forests it rains more than 200 days a year. Sometimes as much as 240 inches of rain falls each year! To give students a feel for the enormous amount of rain forest precipitation, round up a rain gauge (or something similar), some plastic measuring cups, and a supply of paper towels. Place the supplies and a large tub of water in an area of the classroom where students can easily engage in measuring different amounts of water. Each day post a different rainfall-related activity at the measurement center.

In addition have students graph the local rainfall on individual graphs. Local weather stations and/or newspapers can help children keep their graphs up-to-date and accurate. Periodically compare the amount of rainfall in your area to that of a selected rain forest.

A "Tree-mendous" Transformation

Make your journey through the jungle a hands-on event by transforming an area of your classroom into a breathtaking rain forest. Using the information presented in "From Top To Bottom" and other available resources, along with a variety of art materials, make the transformation an ongoing activity. Consider assigning each of four student groups one rain forest layer. Ask each group to be responsible for creating and adding to its assigned layer throughout your rain forest study.

Transformation Tips

Tree trunks: Use cardboard carpet and wrapping-paper rolls in assorted lengths.
Tree foliage and bushes: Supply plenty of crepe paper, tissue paper, bulletin-board paper, and construction paper.
Forest floor: Secure tree trunks in large containers of sand or gravel. Scatter leaf cutouts and scraps of cardboard (decaying wood).
Ferns: Thread several squares of tissue paper onto individual lengths of yarn. Carefully crumple the tissue squares for a lacy effect; then display the resulting fronds in small bunches.
Vines: Twist crepe paper for desired effect.
Flowers: An assortment of tissue paper and construction paper can be used to make colorful blooms.
Inhabitants: Provide references, bulletin-board paper, scissors, markers and crayons, newspaper for stuffing, and a stapler. Students can create a variety of three-dimensional rain forest creatures.

Jungle Journals

As students take part in the rain forest unit you have planned, provide them with a way of capturing their favorite experiences. To do this, give each student a supply of blank paper that has been stapled between two 9" x 12" sheets of white construction paper. Have the youngsters decorate their journal covers. Then, during your rain forest studies, encourage each student to write rain forest–related notes, summarize what he's learned, and describe his favorite activities in his journal. He can also create a bibliography by listing the rain forest books that he reads or that are read to him. In addition, a student can attach desired rain forest memorabilia to his journal pages, such as awards he earns and projects he completes. For added memories, take numerous photographs of students as they work on rain forest–related projects. Distribute the snapshots among your youngsters to be included in the students' journals. At the conclusion of your rain forest studies, each student will have an impressive record of his rain forest experiences and accomplishments.

The Lungs Of Our World

Rain forests help to clean large amounts of carbon dioxide from the air. They also return water and oxygen to the air. For this reason, the green plants in the rain forests are very important for animal life throughout the world. In fact, the rain forests could be called the lungs of our world.

Completing this demonstration will help students understand how green plants release oxygen into the air. Fill a large container with water. Place some water plants (available in ponds or from an aquarium supply store) on the bottom of the container. Lower a wide-mouthed glass jar into the bowl sideways so that the jar fills up with water; then turn the jar upside down so that it covers the plants. Have students observe the results; then place the bowl and jar in a sunny location. After several hours have passed, have students observe the bowl and jar again. This time the youngsters should see air bubbles rising in the water. The air bubbles are caused by the oxygen being given off by the plants—just like oxygen is given off by the trees and plants in the rain forests. If you leave the plants under the jar a while longer, a small pocket of air will form at the top of the jar.

Recycled Rain

Students may be surprised to discover that rain forests help create their own wet climates. This process, called *transpiration,* is made possible by a lush plant population and can be observed by completing the following experiment. Gather a supply of small stones or gravel, potting soil, and a variety of plant cuttings that grow well in wet and warm conditions (spider plants work well). Collect from each student the base from a two-liter soda bottle, a clear plastic sandwich bag, and a tie for the bag.

Each student places a layer of stones in the base of his bottle before adding a two- to three-inch layer of potting soil. Next he plants a plant cutting, making sure that all roots are covered. In turn, have each child water his plant cutting until the soil is moist. Then demonstrate how each child should cover his plant from the base of the stem to the top of the plant with his plastic bag, and use his bag tie to secure the bag at the base of the stem. Place the projects in a warm and sunlit area. After several hours students will witness *transpiration* (water returned to the air via the plants), *condensation* (water droplets forming on the plastic bag), and *precipitation* (drops of water falling to the bottom of the bag).

Rain Forest Gifts

Rain forests are important to people all over the world. In addition to the life-sustaining oxygen that they supply, rain forests are the source of an enormous variety of foods and other products.

Here's a fun way to introduce a variety of rain forest products to your youngsters. In each of several paper lunch bags, place items that are gifts from the rain forest. (Refer to page 131 for a detailed list.) Code the bags so that only you know the contents; then fold and staple the top of each bag closed. Introduce one bag at a time and provide clues to its contents. Ask volunteers to lift, pinch, or smell the bags and share their findings. When the contents of each bag has been identified, remove it from the bag and place it on display. At the conclusion of the activity, students will marvel at the number and diversity of rain forest products. For a fun homework activity, have each child complete a copy of page 131.

On The Wild Side

Though the rain forests of the world are alike in structure, the countless varieties of plants and animals within each forest differ. Scientists have already cataloged 400,000 different species of plants and animals in the world's rain forests. Maybe more amazing is the fact that scientists believe there is an even greater number of rain forest plants and animals yet to be discovered! Encourage students to research rain forest wildlife by setting up an investigation center. Keep a variety of rain forest resource books at the center, along with a supply of report forms (page 132) and a set of colorful markers. Periodically set aside time for your rain forest reporters to share their findings with their classmates. If desired bind the students' reports into a class book entitled "Rain Forest Wildlife."

Pam Crane

Layers Of Learning

These student-made rain forest booklets provide layers of learning. To make a booklet, stack two 9" x 12" sheets of white construction paper and hold the pages vertically in front of you. Slide the top sheet upward approximately two inches; then fold both paper thicknesses forward to create four graduated layers or pages. (See the illustration.) Staple close to the fold; or carefully unfold the papers, staple in the resulting crease, and refold. Have each student illustrate and label the rain forest layers on the cover of his resulting booklet. Facts and/or illustrations relating to specific layers can be recorded under the corresponding flaps.

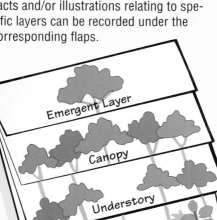

Spreading The Word

Once your students have fallen for the fascinating rain forest wildlife, give them a chance to share information about their favorite plants and animals. For only 20 cents per card and a dose of imagination, your youngsters can create postcards to send to friends and family members. Each card must be cut to legal mailing size, which ranges from 3.5" x 5" to 4.25" x 6". Each student illustrates the front of his card with his favorite rain forest plant or animal. On the back of his card, in the upper left-hand corner, he writes a brief, informative caption about his illustration; then he writes his message and addresses his card just as if it were a commercial postcard. Affix the proper postage and the cards are ready to mail. For extra durability, apply clear Con-Tact® covering to the illustrations before mailing the cards.

For one-of-a-kind Mother's and/or Father's Day gifts, have each student design a series of rain forest postcards, then stack the cards and tie them together with a length of colorful ribbon. What better way for your youngsters to say they care—about their parents and their world!

Spice It Up!

With just a bit of advance preparation you can add a spicy experience to your rain forest activities! For each student you will need a cotton ball and an empty film canister with a snap-on lid. (Most places that develop film are glad to donate these.) Choose five spices and/or flavorings that originate in rain forests. (These include allspice, black pepper, cayenne pepper, chili powder, cinnamon, vanilla, cloves, ginger, nutmeg, and paprika.) Divide the cotton balls into five groups; then sprinkle or dab each group of cotton balls with a different spice or flavoring. Place the scented balls into the canisters and quickly snap the lids in place. Discreetly mark the bottom of each canister to indicate which scent is stored inside.

Distribute one canister to each child. Explain that the canisters contain the fragrances of five different spices and/or flavorings that originate in rain forests. Explain that the object of the game the students are about to play is to find other children in the room who have the same fragrance in their canisters. Have the students suggest how they could go about doing this. Then, on your signal, let the fun begin. Once the groups are formed and verified, ask each group to guess the source of its rain forest fragrance.

Sounds Abound

The appeal of the rain forest can only increase when students discover that in addition to housing a wonderful variety of unique plants and animals, it's also the keeper of a multitude of unusual and exotic sounds! Ask students what kinds of sounds they might hear in a rain forest. List their ideas on the chalkboard. Then, aided by Jane Yolen's book *Welcome To The Green House* (G. P. Putnam's Sons, 1993), take a stroll through a rain forest. "Crinch-crunch"; "a-hoo, ahoo, ahoo"; and "kre-ek, kre-ek, kre-ek" are only a few of the wonderful sound effects included in this lavishly illustrated story. At the conclusion of the book, students will be eager to create a recording of rain forest sounds perfectly suited for their classroom rain forest. "Whup-whup-whoosh!"

Petition Mission

No doubt your youngsters will clamor for a chance to help preserve rain forests and here's a perfect opportunity! Have each student color, personalize, and cut out a construction-paper copy of the rain forest ranger badge on page 133. Laminate the badges for durability if desired; then help each child use a safety pin to attach his badge to his clothing. As a class discuss the plight of rain forests and brainstorm ways people can make a difference in what happens to them. Distribute copies of the rain forest petition on page 133 and urge students to talk with their families and friends about their concerns. Explain that people who share their concern and who are interested in saving rain forests should be asked to sign the petitions. Suggest that students wear their badges as they solicit signatures. Then mail the signed petitions along with a letter composed by the class to:

[Name Of Your State Senator]
U.S. Senate
Washington, DC 20510

Rain Forest Rhapsody

(adapt to the tune of
"Oh Where, Oh Where")

Oh where, oh where have our rain forests gone?
   Oh where, oh where can they be?
With their flowers and forests and fabulous birds,
   Oh where, oh where can they be?

They hold great treasures of trees and plants,
   Of foods and seasonings galore,
And medicines that will fight disease.
   But what if they are no more?

Oh what, oh what can we do to save
   The forests and animals too?
And have the medicines for our ills—
   Well, here is what we can do.

Conserve the products we have right now
   That are made from rain forest wood.
And only purchase our country's beef—
   Yes, that would also be good.

And tell your friends and family
   About our rain forests' plight.
If we work hard to save them now,
   Then things may turn out just right!

Tropical Treats

Whether your students work up an appetite researching the rain forest or you're planning a rain forest rally, keep these recipes handy. All of the ingredients are related to the rain forest in some way!

Rain Forest Mix

Mix together in a large container:
   2 cups peanuts
   2 cups chocolate chips
   2 cups cashew nuts
   2 cups dried banana chips
   2 cups dried papaya
   2 cups Brazil and/or macadamia nuts
   2 cups coconut flakes

Forest Punch

Mix together in a punch bowl:
   2 cups orange juice
   2 cups lemon-lime juice
   2 cups pineapple juice

If desired add a spoonful of lemon sherbet to each cup of punch.

Rain Forest Rally

If you're looking for a unique alternative to a school play that brings parents into the classroom, involves all students, and focuses on academic growth, here's the perfect solution. Make plans to host a rain forest rally! Invite your youngsters' families and friends. The guests of honor can take a guided tour through your student-created rain forest, sample rain forest refreshments, peruse their youngsters' Jungle Journals, and view any other rain forest projects on display. A rousing chorus of "Rain Forest Rhapsody" will definitely be in order. And you might even want to prepare a slide or video presentation for the celebration. It's a wonderful chance for students to share their environmental expertise with their biggest fans!

Name _____

Layers Of Life

Cut out and glue the animals in the rain forest.

Emergent Layer

Toucan
I am brightly colored and very noisy!

Harpy Eagle
I nest in the tallest trees.

Red-Eyed Tree Frog
During the day I hide in the trees and sleep.

Canopy

Three-Toed Sloth
I hang upside down from tree branches.

Understory

Morpho Butterfly
I flit and flutter through the canopy and the understory.

Boa
I slither in the understory and on the forest floor.

Ocelot
I'm a beautiful big cat. I am in danger because people hunt me.

Gecko
I'm a tiny lizard that lives on the forest floor.

Forest Floor

Tapir
My hooves keep me on the forest floor.

Animals shown are from the South American Rain Forest. Animals are not drawn to scale.

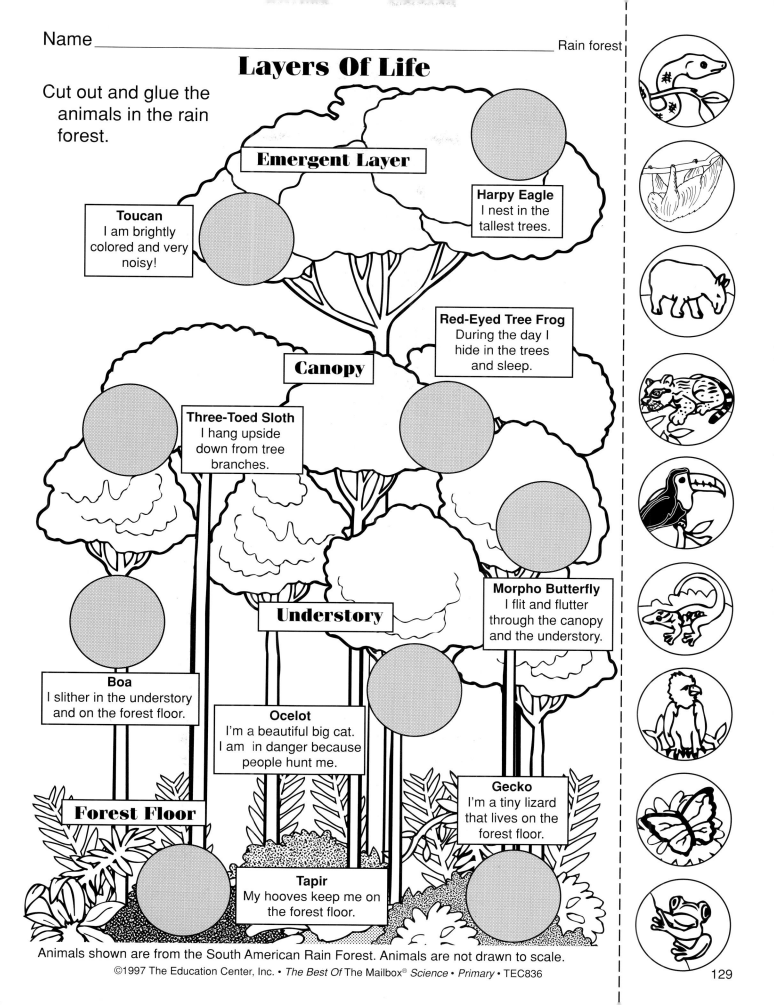

Name _____

Tropical Teasers

Solve each problem on scrap paper.
Write your answer on the line.
Color the animal that has the matching answer.

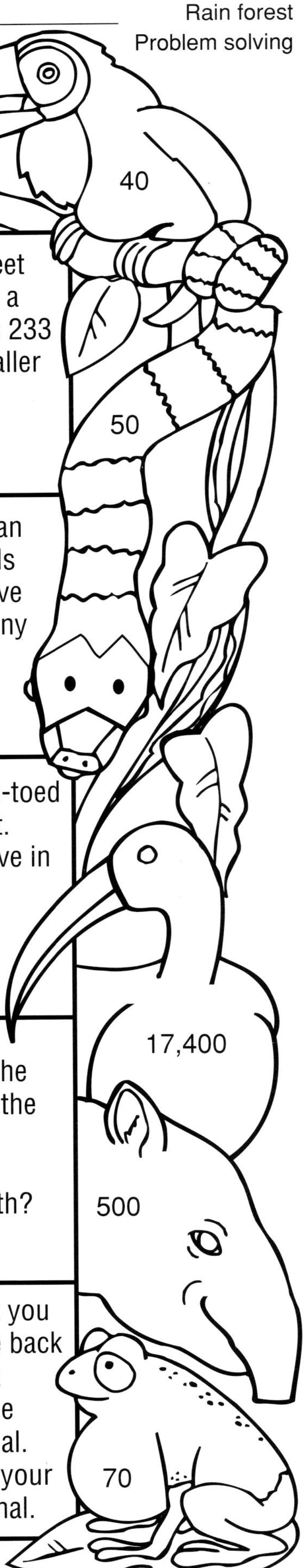

40

4

2,250

1. Each hour 5,800 rain forest acres are destroyed. How many acres are destroyed in 3 hours?

_____ acres

2. 50% of the earth's plants and animals live in the rain forest. What percent do not?

_____ %

3. If 750 trees grow in four square miles of rain forest, how many trees grow in 12 square miles?

_____ trees

4. If one person eats 25 pounds of bananas each year, how many people will 100 pounds feed?

_____ people

5. If each day 100 rain forest species become extinct, how many species will be extinct after 5 days?

_____ species

6. Pretend you are six feet tall. You stand beside a rain forest tree that is 233 feet tall. How much taller is the tree than you?

_____ feet

7. One rain forest tree can have 43 different kinds of ants! If there are five of each kind, how many ants are on the tree?

_____ ants

8. In one minute a three-toed sloth can move 4 feet. How far could he move in ten minutes?

_____ feet

9. Last year about 240 inches of rain fell in the rain forest. If it rains the same amount each month, how many inches fell each month?

_____ inches

10. Find one animal that you did not color. On the back of this sheet, write a teaser that equals the answer on this animal. Have a friend check your work. Color the animal.

50

227

20

215

17,400

500

70

©1997 The Education Center, Inc. • *The Best Of* The Mailbox® *Science* • *Primary* • TEC836 • Key p. 160

Name _____

Made In The Rain Forest

jaguar

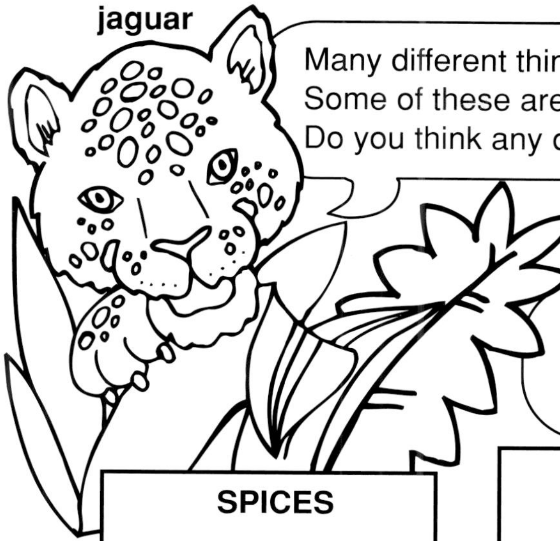

Many different things come from the rain forest.
Some of these are listed below.
Do you think any of these things are in your home?

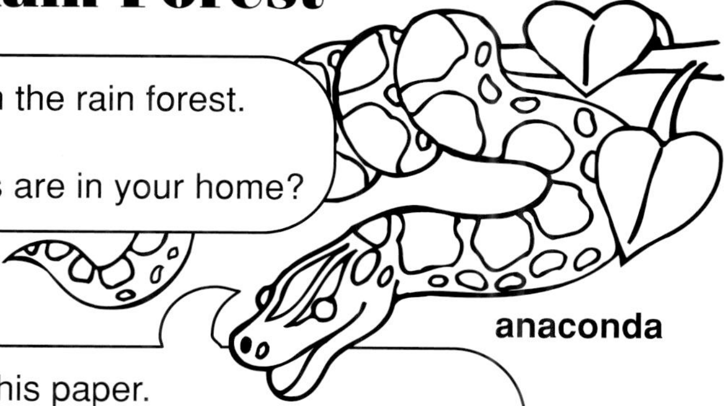

anaconda

Take home this paper.
Ask an adult to help you look for the items.
Draw a check next to each item you find.

SPICES
____ allspice
____ black pepper
____ cardamom
____ cayenne pepper
____ chili powder
____ chocolate/cocoa
____ cinnamon
____ cloves
____ ginger
____ mace
____ nutmeg
____ paprika
____ turmeric
____ vanilla

FRUITS/VEGETABLES
____ avocado   ____ mango   ____ sweet potato
____ banana   ____ orange   ____ tangerine
____ grapefruit   ____ papaya   ____ tomato
____ guava   ____ pineapple   ____ yam
____ lemon   ____ plantain
____ lime   ____ potato

morpho butterfly

OTHER FOODS
____ Brazil nuts   ____ peanuts
____ cashew nuts   ____ rice
____ chicle (chewing gum)   ____ sesame seeds
____ coconut   ____ sugar
____ coffee   ____ tapioca
____ cola   ____ tea
____ macadamia nuts

HOUSEHOLD ITEMS
____ African violet
____ aluminum plant
____ bay rum lotion
____ camphor (insect repellent, medicine)
____ coconut (lotions and soaps)
____ copal (varnish, printing ink)
____ lime (soap, bath oil)
____ patchouli (perfume, soap)
____ rubber (balloons, erasers, foam rubber,
hoses, balls, rubber bands, rubber
gloves, shoe soles, tires)

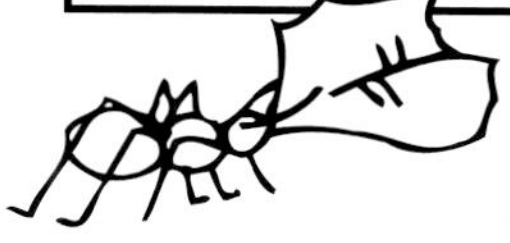

leaf-cutter ants

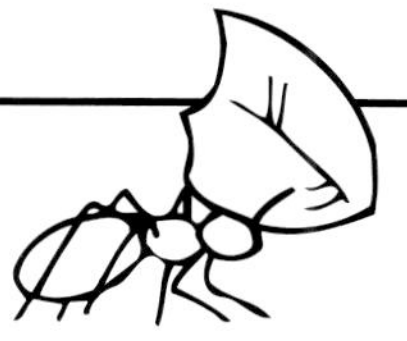

WOODS, CANES, FIBERS
(cabinets, doors, furniture, floors,
models, paneling, toys)
____ balsa
____ bamboo
____ jute (rope, burlap, twine)
____ mahogany
____ rattan
____ teak

Note To Teacher: Use this page with "Rain Forest Gifts" on page 126.

A Rain Forest Plant Report

My report is about a plant called ______

______________________. This plant

grows mostly in the ________________

layer of the rain forest. You can see by

looking at my picture that ____________

______________________________.

One interesting fact about this plant is

____

______________________________.

Another interesting fact is ______________________________

______________________. I think ______________________________

______________________________.

Picture and report by ________________

A Rain Forest Animal Report

My report is about an animal called

______________________. This animal

lives mostly in the ________________

layer of the rain forest. You can see by

looking at my picture that ____________

______________________________.

One interesting fact about this animal is

____

______________________________.

Another interesting fact is ______________________________

______________________. I think ______________________________

______________________________.

Picture and report by ________________

 Note To Teacher: Use with "On The Wild Side" on page 126.

Official Rain Forest Ranger

_____

promises to
**conserve,
promote, and respect**

The Rain Forests
Of The World

©1997 The Education Center, Inc. • TEC836

Rain Forest Rangers To The Rescue!

We, the undersigned, believe that the rain forests are a vitally important resource that must be protected.

We therefore pledge to do all we can do to help preserve the rain forests.

Signature	**Address**

Investigating Tropical Birds

Birds—there are almost 9,000 different kinds. Some birds live on land and others spend almost all their lives at sea. Regardless of where birds live, they all have certain things in common: all birds have beaks or bills, all birds have wings (though not all birds fly), all female birds lay eggs, and all birds have feathers. While it is important to remember these shared characteristics, it is perhaps more amazing to examine the vast differences among birds. And the Tropics—with its colorful assortment of winged inhabitants—is the perfect place to begin your exploration!

A Tropical Habitat

Around the equator lie the Tropics—a hot, wet part of the earth where living things flourish. Much of the Tropics is covered with rain forests. The tall trees of the rain forest are home to a breathtaking variety of plants, birds, monkeys, insects, and other animals. Display a world map during your study of tropical birds. Tape a length of red yarn over the earth's equator and a length of green yarn over both the tropic of Cancer and the tropic of Capricorn. Explain that the Tropics lie on both sides of the equator (red yarn) and are bordered by two more imaginary lines—the tropic of Cancer to the north and the tropic of Capricorn to the south. As different tropical birds are introduced and discussed, ask student volunteers to locate where these birds live on the world map.

Simply Amazing!

Amazing but true—that's the only way to describe the facts included in *Amazing Tropical Birds* by Gerald Legg (Alfred A. Knopf, Inc.; 1991). Unfortunately this Eyewitness Junior Book (Volume 15) is no longer in print. But if you are lucky enough to have a copy in your school or local library, check it out. The book is packed with flocks of fascinating facts about our feathered friends who reside in the Tropics. Other outstanding bird-related resources include:

- *The Bird Atlas* by Barbara Taylor (Dorling Kindersley, Inc.; 1993)
- *Everything You Never Learned About Birds* by Rebecca Rupp (Storey Communications, Inc.; 1995)
- *Outside And Inside Birds* by Sandra Markle (Bradbury Press, 1994)
- *What Is A Bird?* by Robert Snedden (Sierra Club Books For Children, 1993)
- *Our Living World: Birds* by Edward R. Ricciuti (Blackbirch Press, Inc.; 1993)

Rebecca Saunders

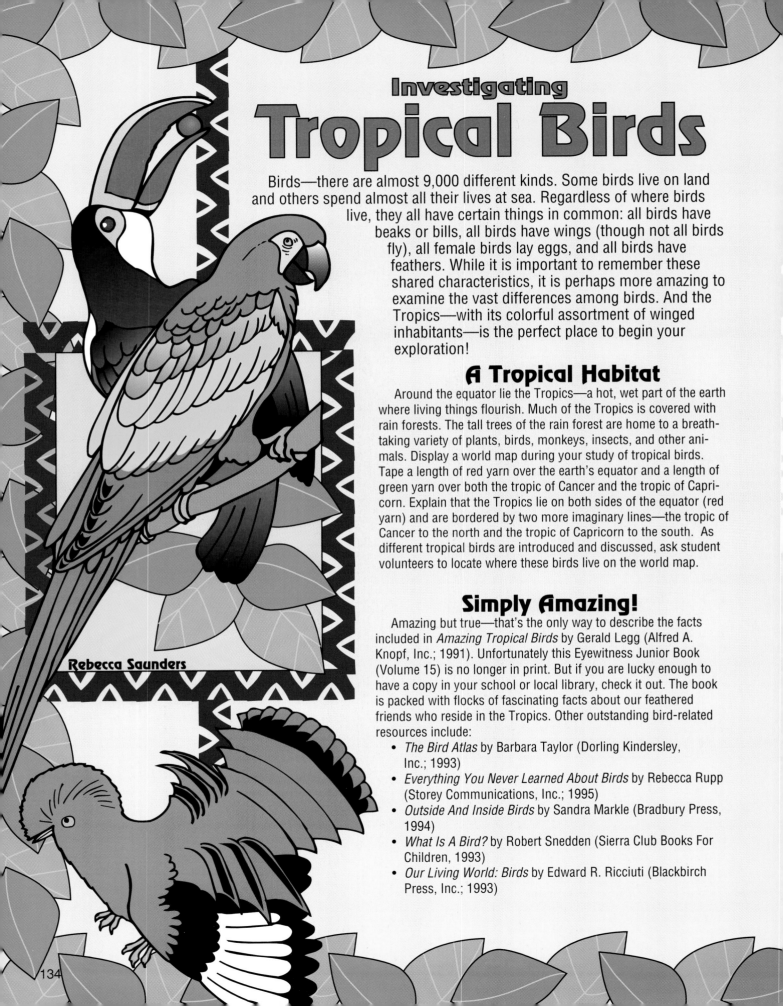

For The Birds

When a student completes this booklet project, she'll have the inside scoop on six different tropical birds and a map of the Tropics, too! Duplicate student copies of page 137 and the fact cards on page 160. Cut a 6" x 30" strip of light-colored bulletin-board paper for each student; then prefold each paper strip into thirds. Have each student use a yellow crayon to color the tropic region on her world map. Next read aloud each of the following descriptions so that students can accurately color the tropical birds on the page. When the coloring has been completed, have students cut out the pieces on both pages.

- Bird #1 is a Resplendent Quetzal. It is mostly bright green except for its deep red belly.
- Bird #2 is a Northern Jacana. It is mostly brown. The wattle between its eyes is yellow. Its beak is yellow too.
- Bird #3 is a Toucan. Toucans are very colorful! Different kinds of toucans have different colors of beaks and faces. Color the beak of this toucan either bright green with a red tip or bright red with a blue tip. The area around its eye can be yellow or blue. Color the rest of its feathers black.
- Bird #4 is a Red-Fan Parrot. It has a brownish head and a green body. Its fan of feathers is red!
- Bird #5 is a Harpy Eagle. It is dark gray with a white belly, a black breast band, and a gray face.
- Bird #6 is a Three-Wattled Bellbird. It has a white head and a brownish body. Its three wattles are black.

To assemble the booklet, place the folded paper strip in front of you. Fold the top flap in half, bringing the paper end to the fold. Pull out the flap that is tucked in the center; then fold this flap in half in a similar manner. (See the illustration.) Keeping the booklet folded, glue the two halves of the world map in place. Unfold the booklet. Match each bird to a fact card. Glue the matching cutouts in the booklet as desired. In the remaining area, write "…The Tropics by [student name]." For a finishing touch, squeeze a trail of glue on the map along the equator. Position one ten-inch length of yarn on each map half so that the extra yarn remains at the center of the booklet. Allow the glue to dry; then fashion a bow from the yarn ends.

(prefolded paper)

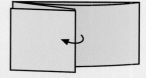

Songs And Calls

One of the ways birds communicate is through *birdsong*. There are two types of birdsong: *calls*—short and simple noises that deliver information, and *songs*—a more complicated and musical type of communication. Birds are born knowing how to call, but a bird must be taught how to sing. Tropical birds have a wide variety of calls and songs. For fun, divide students into small groups and have each group simultaneously repeat one of the following tropical bird's calls!

Bird	Call
Black-Headed Parrot	"KLEEK! KLEEK!"
Toco Toucan	a deep croaking sound
Red-Billed Toucan	a series of rhythmic yelps
Jamaican Tody	a short "cherek"
Hyacinth Macaw	a harsh screech

A Peek At Beaks

The shape of a bird's beak (or bill) provides clues about how or what a bird eats. This student-made booklet project gives youngsters an up close look at the beaks of five different tropical birds. Duplicate student copies of page 138. To make the booklet shown, stack three 4 1/2" x 12" sheets of white construction paper. Slide the top sheet upward about one inch and the bottom sheet downward about one inch. Fold all three paper thicknesses forward to create six graduated pages and staple the resulting booklet close to the fold. Set the booklet aside. Color the birds on your copy of page 138 by referring to the provided color code. Then write your name where indicated and cut on the dotted lines. Glue the title to the top booklet flap. Match each beak description to a tropical bird; then glue the corresponding cutouts in the booklet as shown. Now take another peek at five fabulous beaks!

Shari Abbey—Gr. 3, Abilene Elementary School
Valley Center, KS

Eating Like A Bird

Give your students the inside track on an often misused phrase! The phrase "eats like a bird" is commonly used to describe a light eater. But the fact of the matter is that birds have enormous appetites. Most birds eat one-quarter to one-half of their body weight in food each day! Just imagine if people did that! The diets of tropical birds vary a lot. Many tropical birds eat fruits, nuts, and/or seeds. Other tropical birds feast on insects or flower nectar—or find their food in an ocean, a lake, or a stream. And a few, like the huge Harris's hawk, prey on monkeys and other small animals. So if your students really want to eat like birds, invite each of them to bring to school a serving of dried fruit, sunflower seeds, or a favorite nut. Then mix the ingredients together and let the students senselessly stuff their faces for a few minutes. Now that's eating like a bird!

Fowl Play

In the past 300 years, at least 44 species of birds have become extinct. The greatest threat to birds is pollution and habitat destruction by humans. Many tropical forests are being destroyed at the rate of 100 acres per minute, some environmentalists estimate. Another threat to tropical birds is the growth of the illegal pet trade. Parrots are often captured illegally because they can be sold for large amounts of money. Unfortunately, only about 10 out of each 100 captured parrots live long enough to become pets. Ask students what they think could be done to help save the lives and homes of tropical birds. Then, as a class, investigate what is being done. There are many groups dedicated to helping save the world's rain forests. The Rainforest Action Network (450 Sansome Street, Suite 700, San Francisco, CA 94111) organizes letter-writing campaigns for rain forest preservation. If desired, write a class letter requesting information about a letter-writing campaign in which your students could participate.

Use with "For The Birds" on page 135.

A Peek Inside...
ASIA
EUROPE
AFRICA
AUSTRALIA
ANTARCTICA
NORTH AMERICA
SOUTH AMERICA
Pacific Ocean
Indian Ocean
Atlantic Ocean
Pacific Ocean
Tropic of Cancer
Equator
Tropic of Capricorn

1.
2.
3.
4.
5.
6.

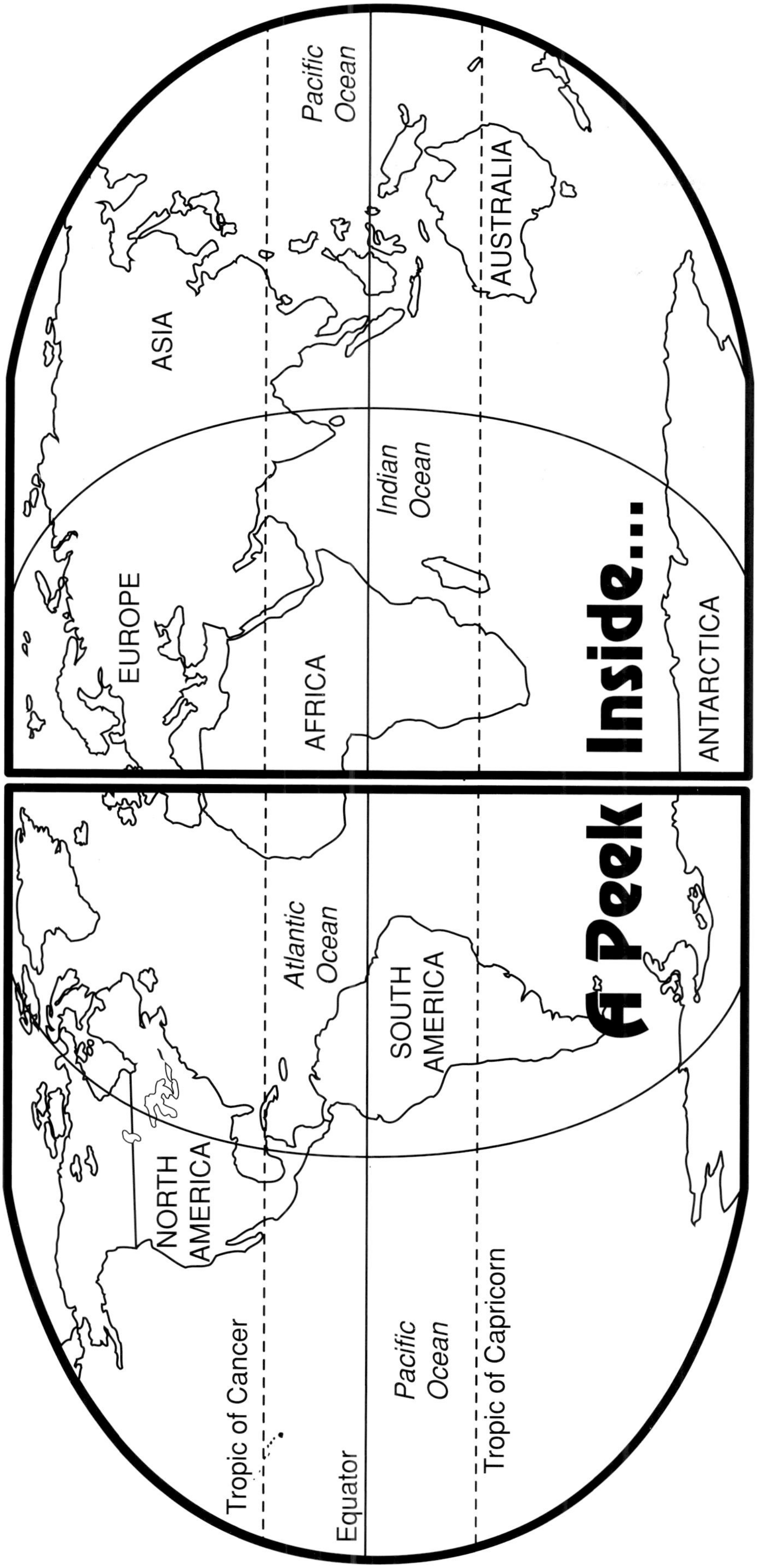

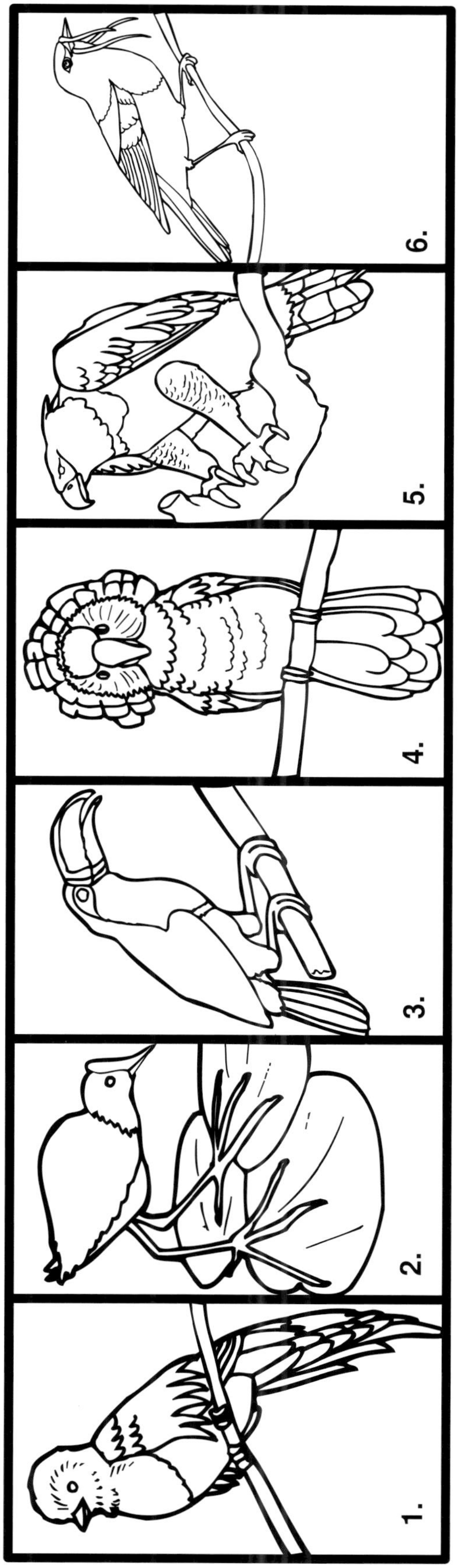

Booklet Project

Use with "A Peek At Beaks" on page 136.

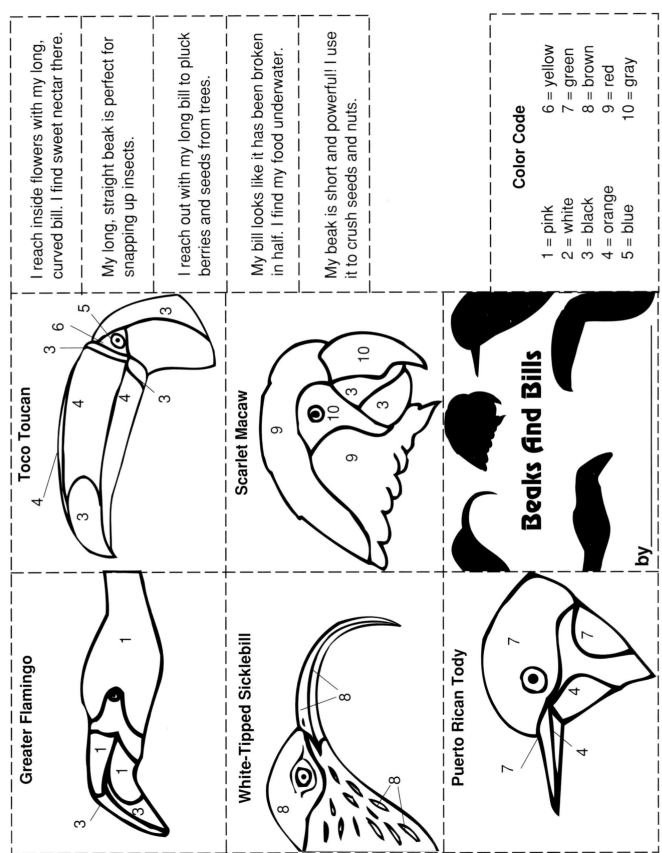

I reach inside flowers with my long, curved bill. I find sweet nectar there.

My long, straight beak is perfect for snapping up insects.

I reach out with my long bill to pluck berries and seeds from trees.

My bill looks like it has been broken in half. I find my food underwater.

My beak is short and powerful! I use it to crush seeds and nuts.

Color Code

1 = pink	6 = yellow
2 = white	7 = green
3 = black	8 = brown
4 = orange	9 = red
5 = blue	10 = gray

Toco Toucan

Scarlet Macaw

Beaks And Bills

by _____

Greater Flamingo

White-Tipped Sicklebill

Puerto Rican Tody

A Pocketful Of Science

Exploring Lift

Watch your youngsters' interest in lift take flight
when you introduce these hands-on activities!

ideas by Ann Flagg

Activity 1: Air Power

Each student will need:

a small spool of thread
a four-inch square of plastic wrap
a rubber band
a sharpened pencil
a thumbtack
a three-inch tagboard square

Directions for the student:

Use the plastic wrap to cover one
end of the thread spool; then use the
rubber band to secure the plastic in
place. Gently poke a sharpened pencil
into the middle of the spool—through
the plastic. Use one hand to hold the
covered end of the spool up to your mouth. Position your
other hand at the opposite end of the spool. Blow air into
the center of the spool.

Question to ask:

1. What happened?

Next:

Demonstrate how to gently poke
the thumbtack into the center of
the tagboard square, invert
the tagboard, and set the
uncovered end of the spool over the protruding end of the
thumbtack. When students have completed these steps, ask
them to predict what will happen when they blow into their
spools. Record their predictions. Then have each student
place his lips over the plastic-covered end of his spool and
blow as hard as he can as he slowly lifts his head. Surprise!
Thanks to air power, the tagboard square rises with the
spool!

More questions to ask:

1. Did the tagboard square behave differently than you
   expected? How?
2. Where did the air go when you blew into the spool?

This is why:

*Moving air exerts less pressure than still air. The air that you
blow through the spool is dispersed at the bottom of the spool—
over the tagboard square. This moving air exerts less air
pressure than the still air below the tagboard. The
still air pressing on the bottom of the
square creates an upward
force called lift.*

Activity 2: More About Moving Air

Each student will need:

a 2" x 11 1/2" paper strip

What to do:

Hold one end of the paper strip just below your lower
lip. Ask students what they think will happen when air is
blown across the paper. Find out how many students
think the unattached end of the paper will move upward
(downward). Then have each student hold her paper strip
as you have modeled and blow hard across the top of the
strip.

Questions to ask:

1. How would you describe the air above (below) the
   paper strip?
2. How is this paper strip similar to the tagboard
   square in Activity 1?
3. Using your knowledge of air power, or *lift,* how do
   you think lift affects the flight of birds? Airplanes?

This is why:

*The moving air above the strip causes a decrease in air
pressure and the still air below pushes the unattached end of the
strip upward—creating lift. It is air flowing over the wings of a
bird that keeps the bird aloft. Birds flap, or move, their wings
forward to make air flow over them. The curved wings of an
airplane help it to sustain lift because the curve forces the air
above the wing to travel faster than the air below the wing. The
principle of lift was first discovered by Daniel Bernoulli.
Bernoulli's principle states that the pressure of a liquid or a gas
decreases as its speed increases.*

139

Pam Crane

Activity 3: Winging It

Each student will need:
a golf-ball-size portion of play dough

What to do:
Challenge each student to use his play dough and his knowledge of lift to mold an airplane wing that—based on its shape—could create lift. Remind students that the air on top of the wing must be forced to move more quickly than the air on the bottom of the wing.

Questions to ask:
1. How does your wing design enable air to move faster on top of the wing than on the bottom of the wing?
2. How do you think people learned about wing design? Why?

This is why:

Students who understand Bernoulli's principle are more likely to design a curved wing. The wing of a bird or an airplane is curved on top and flat on the bottom. The curve on top of the wing forces air to flow up and across the top of the wing. As a result this air must travel farther in the same amount of time as the air traveling beneath the flat bottom of a wing. The faster moving air decreases the air pressure above the wing and lift results. The leading edge of a bird or airplane wing is also thicker than the trailing edge. The thick leading edge causes air to move aside. The thinner trailing edge lets air slip by with less resistance. After people discovered that it is the curved shape of a bird's wing that creates lift, people began to build airplane wings that were slightly curved.

Activity 4: The Wonder Of Wings

Each student will need:
one wing pattern from page 141   a pencil   scissors
tape   crayons

What to do:
Ask each student to color and cut out his wing pattern, fold it on the thin line, and tape the ends of the resulting wing together. Next have each student slide his wing onto his pencil. The taped ends of the wing should hang below the pencil and the curved wing surface should face away from his body. Then, as he grasps each end of his pencil in a different hand, instruct each student to hold the pencil slightly below his lower lip and blow hard across the top of the curved wing surface. Repeat the activity, but this time have each child position his wing so that he blows across the flat wing surface.

Questions to ask:
1. What happened?
2. Why is it important for an airplane wing to be curved on top and flat on the bottom?
3. What else does an airplane (bird) need for flight?

This is why:

Students will discover that blowing across the curved wing surface creates lift, and blowing across the flat wing surface does not. An airplane with inverted wings could not achieve lift. Four basic forces govern flight: lift, gravity (weight), thrust (the power which boosts the bird or plane into the sky), and drag (air resistance, the opposing force of thrust). A correctly designed airplane needs speed and engine power to boost it into the air. A bird relies on its powerful chest muscles to thrust it into the air. However, a heavy bird such as a swan also needs a long runway to build up enough speed to take off.

Wing Patterns

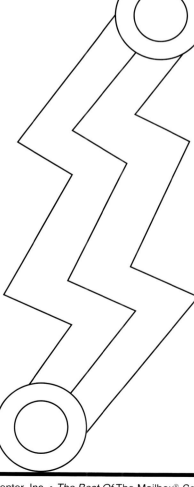

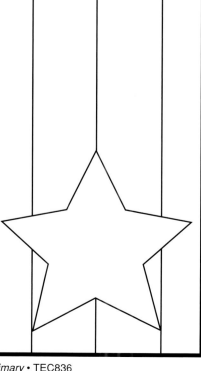

Note To Teacher: Use with "Activity 4: The Wonder Of Wings" on page 140.

A Pocketful Of Science

Getting In Touch With The Ocean

Use the following hands-on activities to "get in touch" with the ocean!

ideas by Ann Flagg

Activity One: Sandy Seashores

You will need:
two rocks per student*
one sheet of white paper per student
spoon
a supply of sand from different locations
five magnets
five hand magnifying glasses

* Rocks of varying hardness yield the best results.

What to do:
Divide students into five groups. Distribute the paper and rocks. Instruct students to gently rub their rocks together over the white paper. After examining their papers, have students trade rocks within their groups and repeat the activity. Continue in this manner as long as desired.

Questions to ask:
1. What do you see on your papers?
2. Did each pair of rocks make the same kind of sand? Why or why not?
3. Has this activity helped you to understand where sand comes from?

Next:
Place a spoonful of sand on each youngster's paper. (Try to vary the types of sand within each group.) Ask students to observe their sand carefully. Then give each group a hand magnifying glass and a magnet. In turn, have students use these objects to find out more about their sand.

Questions to ask:
1. What did you observe?
2. Did everyone in your group observe the same things? Why or why not?

This is why:

Grains of sand were probably once parts of larger rocks. Pounding waves, rushing rivers, freezing water, and chemical reactions between air and water cause rocks to split and break down. Sand may also contain bits of seashells and a variety of minerals. Quartz is the most common mineral found in sand.

Activity Two: Making Waves

You will need:
9" x 13" cake pan
one straw per child
two quarts of water (tinted with blue food coloring)

What to do:
Position the pan on a table; then fill it approximately two-thirds full of tinted water. Distribute the straws. In turn, have each student angle his straw atop the water and blow gently through the straw.

Questions to ask:
1. What happened to the water when you blew through your straw?
2. How could you have made bigger "waves"?

This is why:

The water in our seas and oceans is always moving, even when it looks calm. Winds blowing across the water make ripples or waves on the ocean's surface and create sweeping ocean currents. A wave's size depends on the speed of the wind and how long and how far over the ocean the wind has been blowing. Sometimes huge waves, called tsunamis *or* tidal waves, *are set off by underwater earthquakes and volcanoes.*

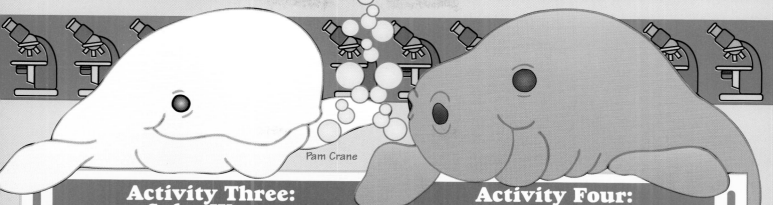

Pam Crane

Activity Three: Salty Water

You will need:

two widemouthed pint jars
raw egg
large serving spoon
three Tbsp. salt
blue food coloring
water
marker
masking tape

In advance:

Without your youngsters' knowledge, fill each jar two-thirds full of water. Use the masking tape and marker to label the jars as "A" and "B". Stir three tablespoons of salt into Jar B. Add a drop of food coloring to each jar and stir.

What to do:

Display the egg and Jars A and B. Ask students to predict what will happen when the egg is lowered into Jar A. Record their predictions on the chalkboard. Ask a student volunteer to use the spoon to lower the egg into the jar.

Questions to ask:

1. What happened to the egg?
2. What do you think will happen when the egg is lowered into Jar B? Why? (Graph these predictions, if desired.)

Next:

Remove the egg from Jar A. Enlist another student volunteer to lower the egg into Jar B.

Questions to ask:

1. What happened to the egg?
2. Why do you think the egg floats in Jar B and not in Jar A?

Next:

Ask a student volunteer to smell the water in each jar. Ask another volunteer to dip a different finger into each jar and taste the liquids. Have these students report their findings.

This is why:

The egg floats in Jar B because the salt in the water increases the density (or thickness) of the water. The salt in our ocean's waters makes it easier for ocean animals to swim. Most of the salt in the ocean is washed from land by rain, then carried by rivers to the oceans. Salt also comes from inside the earth. Material containing salt flows up through the ocean floor. Underwater volcanoes also add salt to the water.

Activity Four: Taking Care Of The Oceans

You will need:

one feather per student (obtainable from craft shops)
one paper towel per student
five small containers partially filled with water
five small containers partially filled with motor oil
five eyedroppers

What to do:

Divide students into five groups. Distribute the paper towels and feathers. Have each student place his feather atop his paper towel.

Questions to ask:

1. What do you think will happen if you place a drop of water on your feather? Why?
2. What do you think will happen if you place a drop of oil on your feather? Why?

Next:

Give each group an eyedropper, a container of water, and another container of oil. In turn, have each student place a drop of water on his feather. Next have each student place a drop of oil on a dry area of his feather.

Questions to ask:

1. What effect did the water have on your feathers?
2. What effect did the oil have on your feathers?
3. Is there oil in our oceans? How does it get there?
4. Do you think this oil is harmful to seabirds and other ocean life?

This is why:

Oil spills threaten marine life. Oil coats things it comes into contact with, which makes it difficult to remove. The oceans are huge, but they are rapidly being polluted by waste materials such as oil. Though most countries now ban the dumping of waste materials at sea (this includes the waste oil often dumped by ships), dumping still occurs, as do accidental oil spills.

Follow-up:

Have students complete the activity on page 144.

The World's Awesome Oceans

Write your opinions on the lines.

 The oceans of the world are very important because _____

_____

_____ .

 The oceans are becoming more and more polluted because _____

_____

_____ .

 Pollution of the world's oceans is harmful because _____

_____

_____ .

 Humans can prevent the oceans from becoming more polluted by _____

_____

_____ .

 If I could spend a day exploring the ocean, this is what I would like to do:

_____

_____

Bonus Box: Glue this paper atop a 9" x 12" sheet of light blue
construction paper. Cut on the dotted lines below and
fold the paper to match the waves on the
top and bottom. Use crayons or
markers to draw a scene
"beneath the waves."

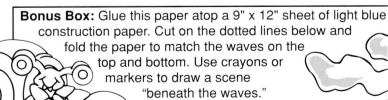

Exploring The Ocean

Make a splash with this collection of ocean-related activities.
What are you waiting for? Dive right in!

ideas contributed by Ann Flagg

Under The Sea

Set the stage for your study of the ocean by transforming your classroom into an ocean paradise. To make the ocean surface, staple blue cellophane to your ceiling, allowing the cellophane to drape and gather in various places. Have students work in co-operative groups to make giant, three-dimensional sea creatures from bulletin-board paper. Suspend the resulting projects from your ceiling with monofilament line.

Judy Barrows—Gr. 3, Valley View Elementary, Abilene, TX

Discovery Journals

As an ongoing project during your ocean study, ask your interning oceanographers to keep discovery journals. To make the journals, duplicate student copies of the journal cover on page 154 onto light blue construction paper. Staple a supply of writing paper between each duplicated cover and a blank sheet of light blue construction paper. Have students decorate their journal covers as desired. Periodically provide time for students to describe their latest ocean discoveries. Or have students write and illustrate undersea adventure stories in their journals.

Wave Watching

Whether your youngsters assist you in making one of these "wave machines" or they make individual ones to keep, this project is going to make a big splash! Remove the label and base from a clear, plastic two-liter soft-drink bottle. (If individual projects are desired, use 20-ounce soft-drink bottles.) Fill the bottle about one-half full of water. Add a few drops of blue food coloring to the water and mix well. Then add mineral oil or baby oil until the bottle is filled. Screw the cap on tightly. (You may wish to tape or hot glue the cap in place to prevent tampering.) When the bottle is turned sideways and rocked gently, the wave motion of the ocean is created. Cool!

Cheryl A. Cerbone & Anna Kiker, Stephen F. Austin Elementary School, Weatherford, TX

Edible Oceans

These eye-catching refreshments will create a wave of excitement among your students! To make this tasty ocean treat, a student spoons soft-set berry blue Jell-O and an assortment of Gummy sea-creature candies into a clear plastic cup. The resulting dessert may be further refrigerated or eaten immediately.

Jana Jensen—Grs. 1 & 2, Sunflower School, Gillette, WY

No Brains!

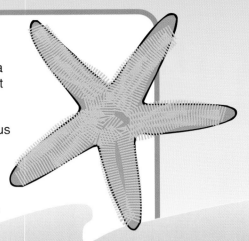

What ocean creature lives in the sea; has five arms, hundreds of feet, and no brains; and cannot swim? A starfish! The starfish or sea star is full of surprises. For example, if a starfish loses an arm, it just grows another one! It also has an unusual way of eating. Instead of bringing food to its stomach, it takes its stomach to the food!

After learning about this unusual creature, students will be anxious to design starfish of their own. To make a textured starfish, cut its shape from colorful construction paper. Use a paintbrush to apply a thin coating of glue to the cutout; then sprinkle crumpled Shredded Wheat atop the glue. Display the completed projects atop a bookcase covered with fishnet, or incorporate them into an ocean mural.

adapted from an idea by Cheryl A. Cerbone & Anna Kiker

Undersea Dioramas

Make a splash with these unique undersea projects. Ask each student to bring two, plastic, two-liter soft-drink bottles from home. (One bottle must be clear.) In advance, for each student, remove the label and cut away the top portion of his clear bottle. Also remove the base from his second bottle and discard the bottle or store it for another project. (See "Wave Watching" on page 145.) To make a diorama, use blue plastic wrap to create a watery backdrop as shown. Then glue or tape cutouts of ocean life to the blue plastic wrap. (Cutouts may be student-created or cut from magazines.) When the ocean scene is finished, fasten the extra base to the top of the project.

Virginia Mozden, South Lincoln Elementary School, Alliance, OH

A Taste Of The Sea

The ocean is an important source of food. Approximately 70 million tons of fish are caught each year. Crabs, lobsters, and seaweed are three of the many other products taken from the sea. Ask your students to brainstorm foods that come from the sea. Then organize a tasting party. To do this, send home a parent letter which asks each youngster to bring five servings of a seafood snack to school on a designated day. Arrange the snacks on a lengthy table and let the snacking begin. Encourage students to sample five different seafood items. At the end of the party, use a safety pin to attach a seafood tasting badge (page 151) to each participant's clothing.

Cheryl A. Cerbone & Anna Kiker

One-Of-A-Kind Sculptures

One can only guess how many sand castles have been crumpled or washed away by waves! Using the following recipe, students can make sand sculptures with staying power. For each batch of moldable sand, mix together in a medium-size pan two cups sand (from a beach or garden center), one cup water, and one cup cornstarch. Stir the mixture over low heat until it thickens. When cool, students can mold the sand into castles, creatures, or other desired shapes. Allow the sculptures to set until they have thoroughly dried. (Note: For best results, mix each batch of moldable sand separately. Doubling the recipe reduces the consistency of the sand mixture.)

Hide-And-Seek

Many ocean animals are skillful hide-and-seek players—their safety and food supply depend on it. By blending in with their surroundings, these creatures can avoid the attentions of their enemies while sneaking up on their prey. Many animals use special patterns or colors as camouflage. Others change their appearance as their surroundings change. Ruth Heller's delightfully illustrated book *How To Hide An Octopus & Other Sea Creatures* (published by Platt & Munk) is an excellent introduction to undersea camouflage.

The booklet project on pages 152 and 153 introduces a few players in this undersea game. Duplicate student copies of both pages on white construction paper. To make a booklet, a student uses the directions on page 152 to color the pictures; then he cuts out each picture. Next he reads the descriptions on the booklet pages (page 153) and glues the corresponding cutouts in the boxes. After completing the booklet cover, he cuts on the dotted lines, then stacks and staples the booklet together.

When I rest on a rock, I become the color of the rock. If the rock is bumpy, I get bumpy too!

Rose Fish
The rose fish doesn't smell bad. It comes in different colors.

Designer Fish

To complete this project, students must apply their knowledge of undersea camouflage. To begin have each student glue an eight-inch square of wallpaper near the top of a 9" x 12" sheet of light blue construction paper. Next give each youngster a white construction-paper copy of the fish pattern on page 151, and explain that these fish must live in the "wallpaper environments" the students have created. Tell students that before they glue their fish into their new homes, they should decorate the fish in such a way that they will be safe from their predators. Finally have each student write the name of his fish and two interesting facts about it near the bottom of his project. Provide time for students to share their unique fish with their classmates.

The Sea Is A House For Me

Culminate your ocean studies with this big-book activity. First read aloud *A House Is A House For Me* by Mary Ann Hoberman (published by Viking Penguin, Inc.). This delightfully silly picture book explores countless houses that host a variety of unusual inhabitants. At the conclusion of the book, write a student-generated list of homes found on the seashore or in the sea. Your list might include "a seashell is a home for a hermit crab," "an oyster is a home for a pearl," "a tide pool is a home for a starfish," and "a beach is a home for driftwood." When your list is complete, have students (working individually or in small groups) copy and illustrate the phrases on large sheets of paper. Compile the booklet pages between a student-decorated cover entitled "The Sea Is A House For Me."

Susan Nixon—Gr. 1, Cartwright School, Phoenix, AZ

Diving Into Literature

Create a wave of reading enthusiasm with these ocean-related books and the activities that accompany them.

books reviewed by Deborah Zink Roffino

Whale Is Stuck
Written by Karen Hayles & Illustrated by Charles Fuge
Published by Simon & Schuster

Meet several of the ocean's northernmost inhabitants in this delightful adventure about a whale who finds himself stranded on an ice floe. A menagerie of helpful friends including Narwhal, Seal, Polar Bear, and Walrus struggle valiantly to move the gigantic mammal. But the whale's friends need a little "break" from Mother Nature to get the job done.

To help students better understand the enormous task that Whale's friends had undertaken, assemble students in the hallway or on the playground, and have them unwind a length of yarn or string that is approximately 100 feet in length. Explain that a blue whale may be up to 100 feet in length and weigh up to 120 tons—which equals the weight of approximately 25 elephants or 1,800 people! Wow, what a whale!

Coral Reef
Written by Barbara Taylor
Photographed by Jane Burton
Published by Dorling Kindersley, Inc.

Larger-than-life photographs and enlightening text introduce young readers to the animals and plants of the coral reef. Dive into a watery world full of dazzling colors and shapes. It's an underwater tour that leaves a lasting impression!

While students may not totally understand the hows and whys of coral and coral reefs, they will undoubtedly be impressed by the beauty these gardens contribute to our world's oceans and seas. Corals come in wonderful colors and shapes—with delightful names like "dead man's fingers," "brain coral," and "fan coral." Students will enjoy illustrating and naming yet-to-be-discovered corals. Using crayons, have each student draw and color a coral (and other desired undersea life) on the bottom half of a 9" x 12" sheet of light blue construction paper. Then have him write the name of his coral and one sentence describing it on a half-sheet of writing paper. Have each student assemble his work as shown. Compile the completed projects in a class booklet entitled "Coral Creations."

Big Toe Coral
This colorful coral looks like a big toe, but it doesn't smell like one!

Rivers And Oceans

Written by Barbara Taylor
Published by Kingfisher Books

Covering all the waters of the earth, this small, fact-filled book has several excellent sections on oceans, seas, tides, currents, and waves. Illuminating pictures and photographs accompany the keen text. Simple experiments are suggested to help explain water phenomena—glaciers, erosion, the water cycle, and more—for children.

Most of the world's water is contained in its five oceans: the Arctic, Atlantic, Indian, Pacific, and Antarctic. With just a few globes borrowed from neighboring classrooms, students can easily examine the oceans in small groups. After each ocean has been located, have students determine which is the largest ocean (Pacific) and the smallest ocean (Arctic). Next have students locate the world's seas. Help students conclude that seas are much smaller than oceans and that they are usually found close to, or surrounded by, land.

The Rainbow Fish

Written & Illustrated by Marcus Pfister
Published by North-South Books

Rainbow Fish, with his shimmering scales, is quit aware that he is the most beautiful fish in the sea. And because of his vanity, he soon becomes the loneliest fish in the deep blue ocean. A bit of sound advice from a wise octopus helps Rainbow Fish discover the real value of personal beauty and friendship.

For a fun follow-up activity to this charming story, create these eye-catching friendship posters. First have each youngster glue a small scale shape cut from holographic gift wrap near the center of a 4 1/2" x 6" sheet of white construction paper. Then, using crayons, a student designs a colorful fish around the scale and cuts out his completed project. Next divide students into small groups and have each group brainstorm a list of friendship tips. After a group has chosen its five favorite tips, give the group a black marker and a sheet of light blue poster board labeled "Friendship Tips." One group member writes the tips on the poster board while the remaining members use construction-paper scraps to create assorted underwater decorations. Finally have the students glue their fish projects and decorations to their group's poster. Display the completed projects in prominent locations around the school.

Friendship Tips
- be polite
- share
- help each other
- listen to each other
- be honest with each other

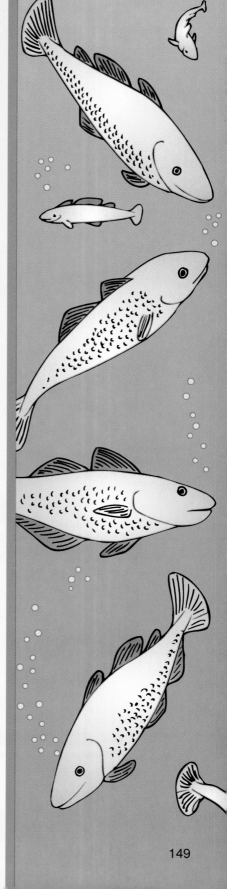

More Books To Use With Your Ocean Unit

The Magic School Bus On The Ocean Floor
Written by Joanna Cole & Illustrated by Bruce Degen
Published by Scholastic Inc.

Sam The Sea Cow
Written by Francine Jacobs & Illustrated by Laura Kelly
Published by Walker And Company

A House For Hermit Crab
Written & Illustrated by Eric Carle
Published by Picture Book Studio

How To Hide An Octopus & Other Sea Creatures
Written & Illustrated by Ruth Heller
Published by Platt & Munk, Publishers

Fish Eyes: A Book You Can Count On
Written & Illustrated by Lois Ehlert
Published by Harcourt Brace Jovanovich

Is This A House For Hermit Crab?
Written by Megan McDonald & Illustrated by S. D. Schindler
Published by Orchard Books

Swimmy
Written & Illustrated by Leo Lionni
Published by Pantheon

The Whales' Song
Written by Dyan Sheldon & Illustrated by Gary Blythe
Published by Dial Books For Young Readers

The Smallest Turtle
Written & Illustrated by Lynley Dodd
Published by Gareth Stevens, Inc.

Ask me
about
our
Seafood Feast!

Use badge with "A Taste
Of The Sea" on page 146.

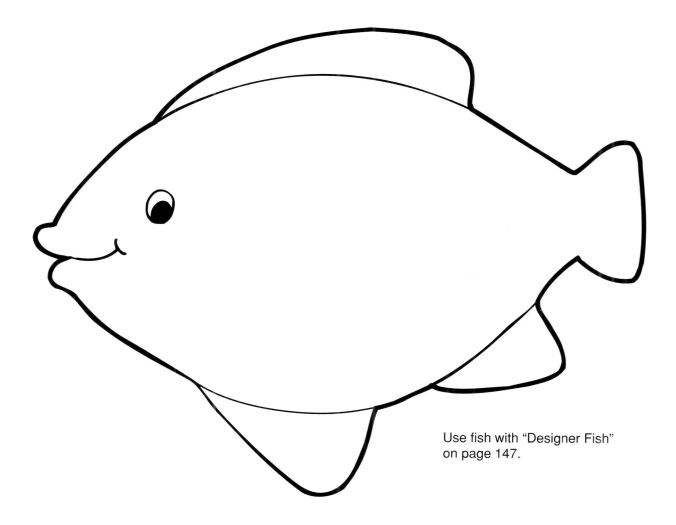

Use fish with "Designer Fish"
on page 147.

Trumpet Fish

☐ Color the coral bright purple.
☐ Color the fish purple.
☐ Color the rest of the picture.

Octopus

☐ Color the rocks and the octopus the same color.
☐ Color the rest of the picture.

Peacock Flounder

☐ Color the rings on the fish blue.
☐ Color the fish light brown.
☐ Color the sand light brown.
☐ Color the rest of the picture.

Copperband Butterfly Fish

☐ Color the fish's stripes bright yellow.
☐ Color the fish's eye black.
☐ Color the circles near the tail black.
☐ Color the rest of the picture.

Clown Triggerfish

☐ Color some of the fish's spots blue.
☐ Color some spots yellow.
☐ Color the fish gray.
☐ Color the rest of the picture.

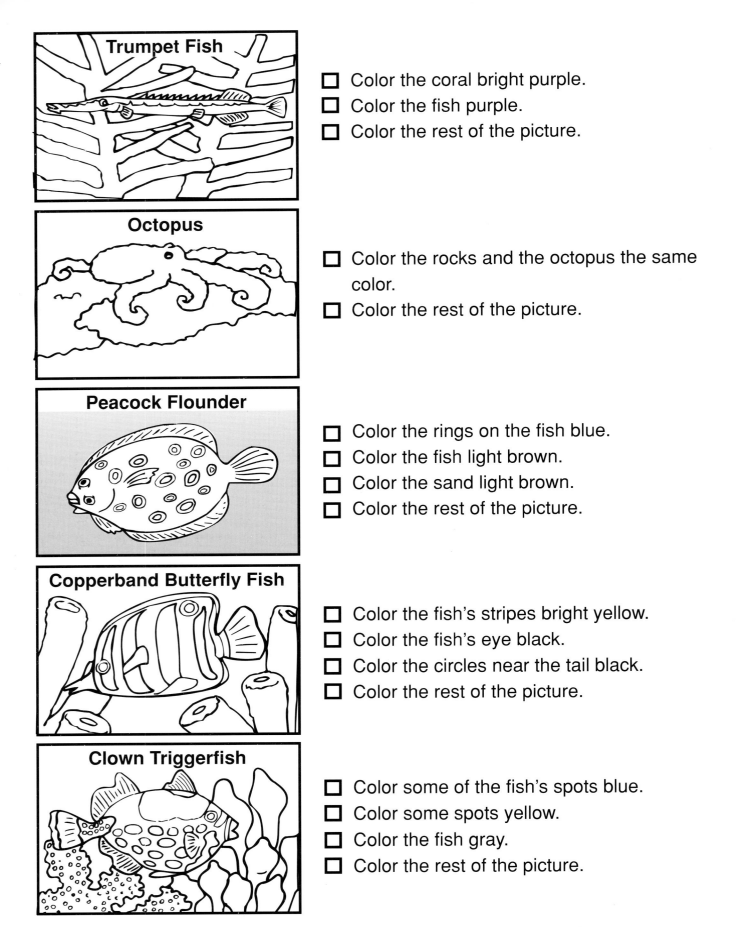

Note To The Teacher: Use with "Hide-And-Seek" on page 147. Suggest that students check the boxes as they complete the corresponding directions.

Name_____

Undersea Hide-And-Seek

The false eye spot on my tail confuses my enemies. When an enemy snaps at the eye spot, I swim away.

To hide, I lie on the ocean floor and flick sand over myself. I can see my enemies, but they can't see me.

It is easy for me to hide in a coral reef. I just become the same color as the coral.

My spots are many different sizes. They are different colors, too. This confuses my enemies.

When I rest on a rock, I become the color of the rock. If the rock is bumpy, I get bumpy too!

Note To The Teacher: Use with "Hide-And-Seek" on page 147.

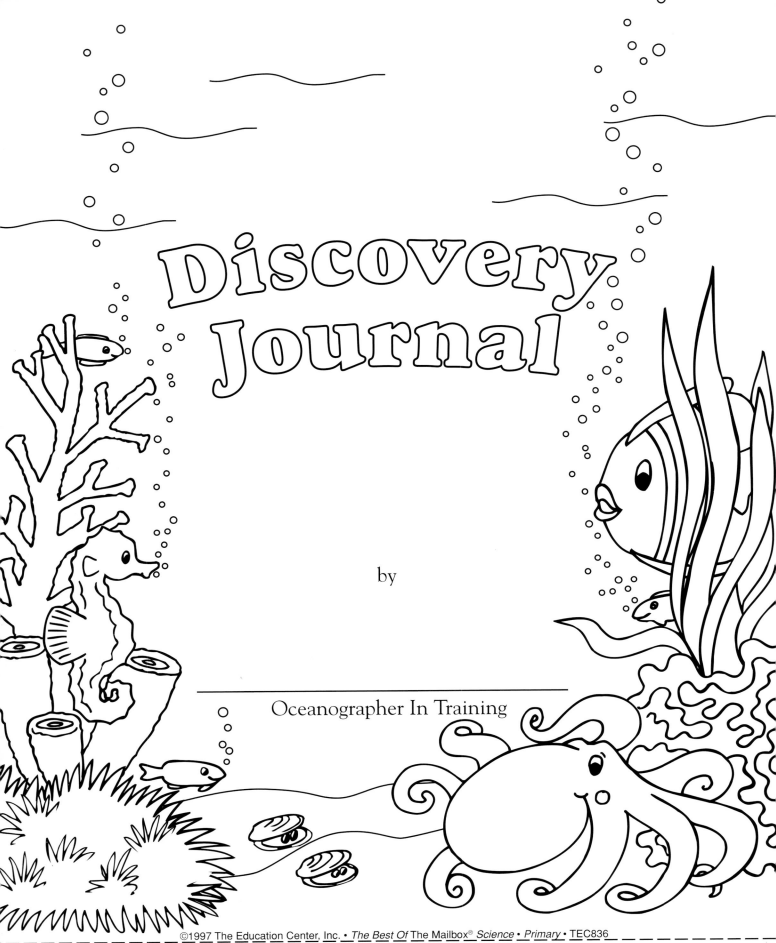

Discovery Journal

by

_____

Oceanographer In Training

Note To The Teacher: Use with "Discovery Journals" on page 145. Or white-out the programming and use the page for a parent letter or
a variety of student activities.

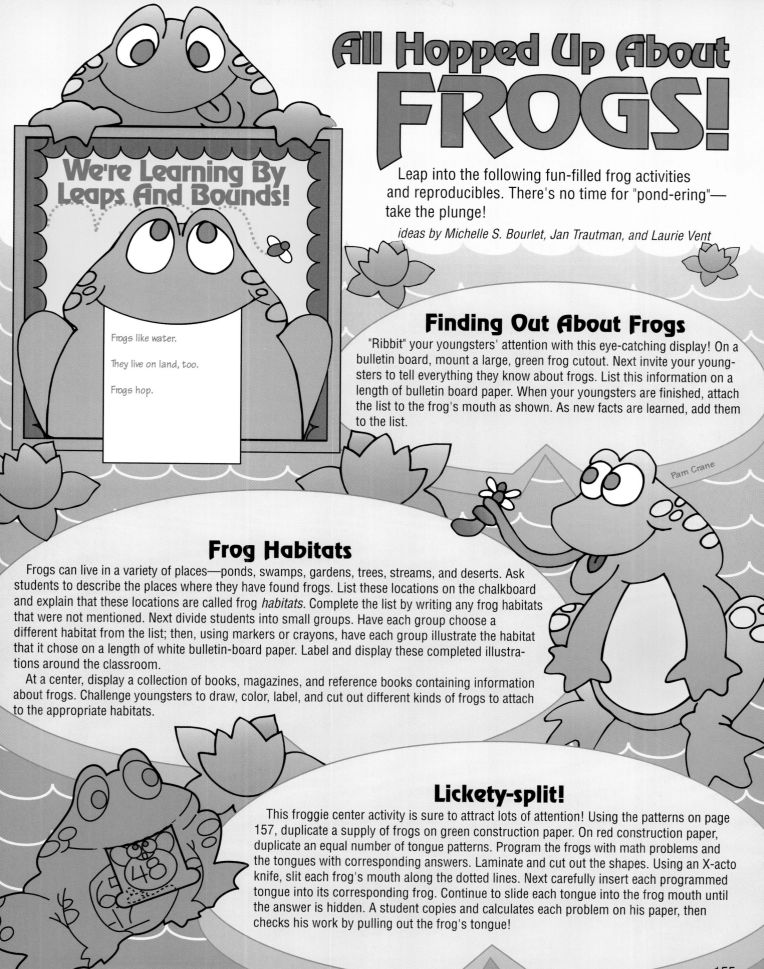

All Hopped Up About FROGS!

Leap into the following fun-filled frog activities and reproducibles. There's no time for "pond-ering"—take the plunge!

ideas by Michelle S. Bourlet, Jan Trautman, and Laurie Vent

We're Learning By Leaps And Bounds!

Frogs like water.

They live on land, too.

Frogs hop.

Finding Out About Frogs

"Ribbit" your youngsters' attention with this eye-catching display! On a bulletin board, mount a large, green frog cutout. Next invite your youngsters to tell everything they know about frogs. List this information on a length of bulletin board paper. When your youngsters are finished, attach the list to the frog's mouth as shown. As new facts are learned, add them to the list.

Pam Crane

Frog Habitats

Frogs can live in a variety of places—ponds, swamps, gardens, trees, streams, and deserts. Ask students to describe the places where they have found frogs. List these locations on the chalkboard and explain that these locations are called frog *habitats*. Complete the list by writing any frog habitats that were not mentioned. Next divide students into small groups. Have each group choose a different habitat from the list; then, using markers or crayons, have each group illustrate the habitat that it chose on a length of white bulletin-board paper. Label and display these completed illustrations around the classroom.

At a center, display a collection of books, magazines, and reference books containing information about frogs. Challenge youngsters to draw, color, label, and cut out different kinds of frogs to attach to the appropriate habitats.

Lickety-split!

This froggie center activity is sure to attract lots of attention! Using the patterns on page 157, duplicate a supply of frogs on green construction paper. On red construction paper, duplicate an equal number of tongue patterns. Program the frogs with math problems and the tongues with corresponding answers. Laminate and cut out the shapes. Using an X-acto knife, slit each frog's mouth along the dotted lines. Next carefully insert each programmed tongue into its corresponding frog. Continue to slide each tongue into the frog mouth until the answer is hidden. A student copies and calculates each problem on his paper, then checks his work by pulling out the frog's tongue!

From Eggs To Frogs

Using a variety of illustrated resource books, explore the development of a frog. One excellent resource is *Tadpole And Frog* by Christine Back and Barrie Watts (Silver Burdett Company, 1986). Then follow up your research with this hands-on activity.

Using the wheel pattern on page 157, duplicate one white and one green construction-paper wheel for each youngster. To make a picture wheel, first color the illustrations on the white copy of the wheel. Next cut out both wheels. Cut one triangular section from the green wheel; then place the green cutout atop the white wheel so that the programming on both cutouts faces inward. To attach the two cutouts, insert a brad through the center of both. If desired, attach a tissue paper flower atop the resulting "lily pad wheel cover." To make the flower, attach individual squares of white and lavender tissue paper that have been wrapped around the end of a pencil and dipped in glue. When the projects are complete, pair students and let each youngster explain the different stages in a frog's development by using his picture wheel.

Freeze Frog

Take a break from your regular routine to play this modified version of freeze tag. Students will jump at the chance! Designate an area of your playground to be "the pad." Choose one student to be It and instruct all other students to be "frogs." When a frog is tagged outside the pad, he must freeze and remain motionless until he is tapped by a mobile frog. When all of the frogs are frozen or after a predetermined amount of time has passed, select a new It. For added fun, require each It to identify himself as one of the frog's natural enemies.

Paper Plate Frogs

Have youngsters create a pond full of croakers using these directions. To make a frog, use green tempera paint to sponge print the outside of a paper plate. Copy the patterns on page 158 onto green construction paper; then cut out the patterns. Trace a second eye and front leg shape onto a 4" x 9" piece of green construction paper; then cut out the resulting shapes. Decorate the eye cutouts using scraps of white and black construction paper. When the painted plate has thoroughly dried, glue the pieces around the plate as shown. Then, using a black permanent marker, draw a large smile on the frog. If desired, wrap a 1/2" x 6" strip of pink construction paper around a pencil; then remove the strip and attach one end of it to the frog's mouth.

A Froggie Finale

Plan a froggie finale and watch your youngsters jump for joy! During this closing celebration, invite students to share what they found most interesting about frogs, stories or reports that they wrote about frogs, and books featuring frog (and/or toad) characters that they read. For refreshments, serve each youngster a celery stick that has been filled with peanut butter and adorned with raisins (flies on a log) and a frog float. To make a float, partially fill a paper cup with 7-Up®; then float a scoop of lime sherbet in the liquid. Decorate the scoop of sherbet with two chocolate chip "eyes."

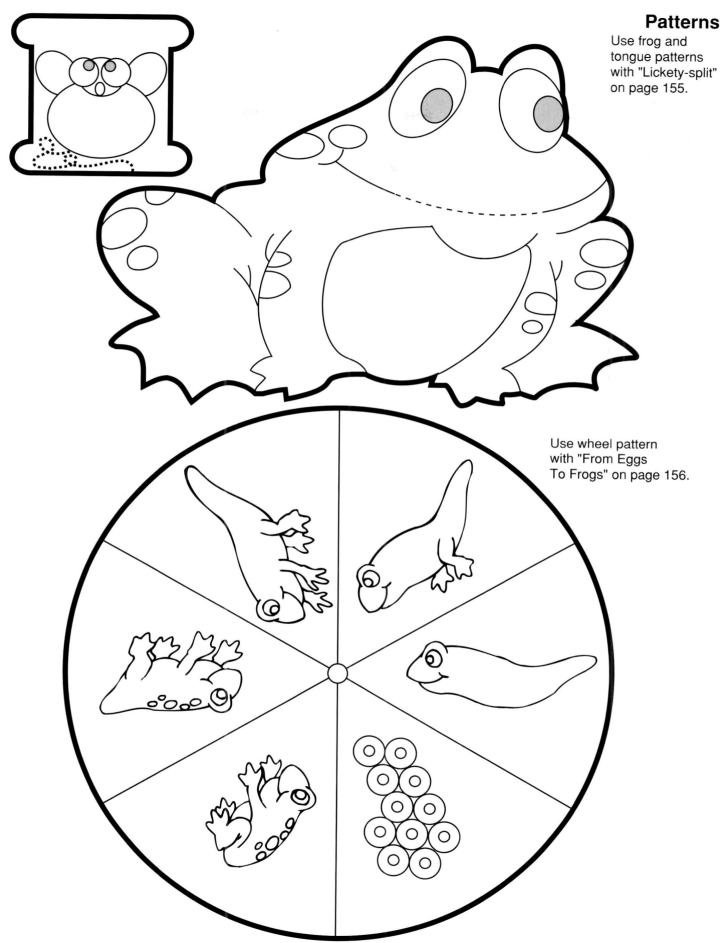

Patterns

Use frog and tongue patterns with "Lickety-split" on page 155.

Use wheel pattern with "From Eggs To Frogs" on page 156.

Patterns

Use with "Paper Plate Frogs"
on page 156.

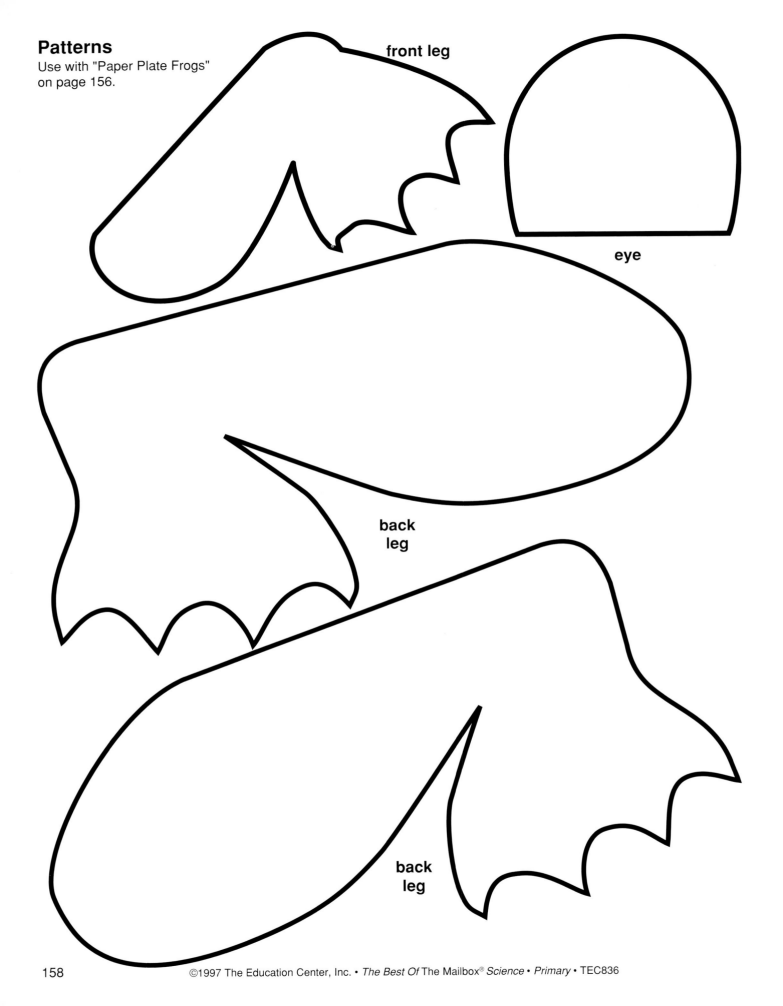

front leg

eye

back
leg

back
leg

Answer Keys

Page 32

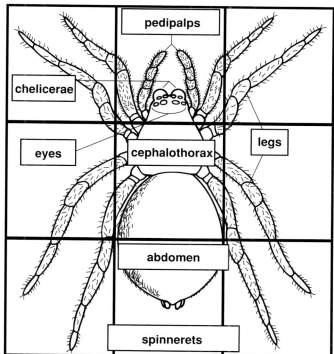

Page 47

1. king penguin
2. king penguin, emperor penguin
3. 25 inches
4. chinstrap penguin
5. little blue penguin
6. 30 inches taller
7. chinstrap penguin
8. Yes. It is 15 inches taller.

Page 50

A	B	C
tobogganing	rookery	porpoising
crèche	brood pouch	waddling
krill	molting	

Page 93 (Order of answers may vary.)

Facts About Weather

Water evaporates more quickly in the sun.
A tornado can cause a lot of damage.
There are many different kinds of clouds.
Lightning is very dangerous.
The weather affects how people dress.

Opinions About Weather

Summer weather is the best weather.
Everyone feels sad when it rains.
Forecasting the weather is fun.
A foggy night is scary.
Snowflakes are beautiful.

Page 94

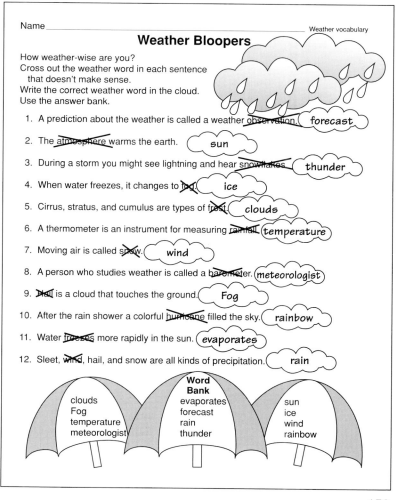

Answer Keys

Page 105

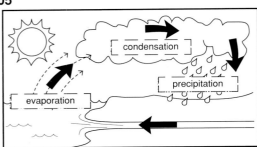

The sun heats the earth's water.	
The warmed water turns into vapor and rises in the air.	
As the water vapor rises, it cools down.	
The cooled water vapor forms tiny droplets of water.	
The tiny water droplets form clouds.	
In the clouds the tiny water droplets join together.	
The water droplets become heavy.	
The heavy droplets fall to the earth as rain, snow, sleet, or hail.	

Page 130

1. 17,400 acres
2. 50%
3. 2,250 trees
4. 4 people
5. 500 species
6. 227 feet
7. 215 ants
8. 40 feet
9. 20 inches
10. Answers will vary.

Page 116: Desert Wildlife Locations

Gila monster	=	North American deserts
saguaro cactus	=	only in the Sonoran Desert
oryx	=	Arabian Desert and deserts in Africa
jerboa	=	deserts in Asia and Africa
camel	=	The one-hump camel shown is a *dromedary camel.* It is native to the hot deserts of Arabia and North Africa, but it has also been introduced to parts of America and Australia. The two-hump camel (not shown on the map) is called a *Bactrian camel.* It is native to the cooler central Asian deserts.
emu	=	deserts in Australia

Fact Cards

Use with "For The Birds" on page 135.

Resplendent Quetzal	**Northern Jacana**	**Cuvier's Toucan**
I am the national bird of Guatemala. My green tail feathers can be two feet long!	My extralong toes allow me to walk on floating plants without sinking! Some people call me a *lily-trotter.*	I am very playful. Sometimes I use my colorful beak to toss fruit to other toucans.
Red-Fan Parrot	**Harpy Eagle**	**Three-Wattled Bellbird**
When I get excited, I spread my red crest into a broad fan. Sometimes I use my feet to put food in my beak.	Beware! I am fearsome and I can fly 50 miles per hour.	I have a big mouth! I can swallow large fruits and I have a very loud call!